ALSO FROM GIFF CONSTABLE AND FRANK RIMALOVSKI

Talking to Humans is the award-winning bestseller that teaches you the essentials of customer discovery, an indispensable skill for vetting and improving any new startup or innovation. This companion book to *Testing with Humans* explains how to structure and run effective customer interviews, find candidates, and turn learnings into action.

Acclaim for *Testing with Humans*

"Answering the question of 'What do you do after you get out of the building?' *Testing with Humans* is a 'must have' book for entrepreneurs."
**–Steve Blank, author of The *Startup Owners Manual*
and *Four Steps to the Epiphany***

"*Testing with Humans* is the ideal follow-up to Constable and Rimalovski's *Talking to Humans*. It literally takes what they've already taught us to the next level--from customer discovery to experimenting with those customers in order to find product-market fit. All the steps for designing, building, and launching experiments are here, along with a host of examples and great advice born of real experience."
–Eric Ries, author of *The Lean Startup* and *The Startup Way*

"A brilliant blend of principles, examples, templates and checklists on a topic that is so essential to entrepreneurs. This book makes you want to get out of the building and run experiments even if you are not working on a startup!"
–Singari Seshadri, Head of the Stanford University Venture Studio

"*Testing With Humans* explains the scientific method to explore the biggest unknowns in your business. It provides the essential tools to critically test your hypothesis on the most difficult test subject known to man, namely man."
–Errol Arkilic, Founding Program Director, NSF I-Corps & CEO, M34 Capital

"Giff has distilled down years of learnings into quite a useful package. If you're looking to get better at testing and validating ideas in the shortest amount of time (who isn't?!), this is the book for you."
–Hiten Shah, Co-Founder of KISSMetrics, CrazyEgg, and Product Habits

"Every entrepreneur should read *Testing with Humans* and keep it nearby. It is an outstanding combination of readability, rigor and concrete action items for one of the most important and challenging things every entrepreneur must do - define the right hypotheses, properly test them and maximize the learning in the process."

–Professor Bill Aulet, MIT, author of
Disciplined Entrepreneurship

"Entrepreneurs all know that they should talk to customers and run experiments, but that is easier said than done. This book does an excellent job making these concepts concrete and actionable."

–Beth Ferreira, Partner at FirstMark Capital

"From my classroom at Carnegie Mellon to the boardroom of my VC investments, this book will join *Talking to Humans* as a critical resource helping those teams validate their ideas."

–Sean Ammirati, VC and author of *The Science of Growth*

"*Testing with Humans* is a must read for every product team that wants to build the right thing. It's a practical guide to experimentation, clearly explaining many types of experiments and breaking down exactly how to run them."

–Melissa Perri, author of *The Build Trap*

"Giff and Frank have done it again. This practical, tactical book explains — to entrepreneurs, product managers and veteran practitioners alike — why you need to run experiments, how to do it and what to do with what you learn. It's direct, concise and immediately useful. Read it this morning. Run your first experiment this afternoon."

–Jeff Gothelf, author of *Sense & Respond* and *Lean UX*

"*Testing with Humans* is 70% practical, 30% inspirational, and 100% of it is stuff I wish I'd known 20 years ago."

–Jeff Patton, author of *User Story Mapping*

"Entrepreneurs need confidence, but not arrogance. Entrepreneurial arrogance is an early warning sign of impending doom. Entrepreneurial confidence is based on an inquiring mind, that has beliefs, and is open to testing them. In this book Constable and Rimalovski guide us on a learning journey to test our entrepreneurial assumptions - the key to gaining true entrepreneurial confidence, mitigating risks and moving forward toward success."

–Jerome Engel, U.C. Berkeley and Founding National Faculty Director, NSF I-Corps

"*Testing with Humans* fills a much-needed gap in the Lean Startup and innovation strategy world. Many espouse evidence-based testing approaches, but easier said than done — or taught. Until now."

–Edmund Pendleton, Lead Instructor NSF and NIH I-Corps

Table of Contents

Introduction

"In general we look for a new law by the following process: first we guess it. Don't laugh — that's really true. Then we compute the consequences of the guess to see what, if this law is right, what it would imply. Then we compare those computation results to nature, i.e. experiment and experience. We compare it directly to observation to see if it works.

If it disagrees with experiment, it's wrong. That simple statement is the key to science. It doesn't make a difference how beautiful your guess is, it doesn't make a difference how smart you are, who made the guess or what his name is — if it disagrees with experiment, it's wrong. That's all there is to it."

RICHARD FEYNMAN
Physicist

WHY THIS BOOK?

To successfully pull off a startup, you need more than grit and perseverance. You have to nail the vision, timing and execution. Get any one of those wrong, and you're left with little more than hard lessons and wasted time and money. Vision comes first, but you've also got to get the details right across your entire business model: your choice of initial target customer, revenue and pricing model, customer acquisition approach and channels, product design and creation, and much more. Before you rally a team, raise money, or move heaven and earth to bring a company into being, wouldn't you want to de-risk your vision, timing and execution? There are two great places to start: talking to your potential customers and running experiments.

In 2014, Frank and I published *Talking to Humans*, aimed at the first of those two. Our goal was to help entrepreneurs learn how to speak directly with potential customers in order to vet and hone their ideas — what the startup world now calls "customer discovery". Little did we know that the book would be read by many tens of thousands of people and picked up by leading universities, accelerators, the National Science Foundation's I-Corp program, and companies across the USA and around the world.

But customer discovery is not enough on its own. Talking with other people will give you the strongest leaps of inspiration and understanding, but experiments give you the strongest proof. An experiment is a test designed to help you answer the questions "Should we do this?" or "Am I right about this?" If you are open to learning, the insights from your experiments will help you refine your creation and improve your odds of success.

Oddly enough, this isn't the way creative and entrepreneurial brains typically like to work. Instead, we imagine a desired future, we design what needs to happen to bring that future about, and we are then blazingly impatient to get going and bring that future about.

That combination of conviction and impatience is an incredible strength for an innovator, but it is also a devilish saboteur. After all, if you run really fast in the wrong direction, you are further from your goal.

WHAT'S IN THE BOOK

Experiments come in all shapes and sizes, but this book is about experiments designed to validate (or invalidate) new product and business ideas. This will be particularly, but not exclusively, applicable to startups, product teams, and innovation teams. Like *Talking to Humans*, this book is a concise, practical primer. It begins with a fictional story of two engineers-turned-entrepreneurs, and then shifts into a mix of tactics and theory on designing and running experiments. We also talk about how to foster more of a culture of experimentation within your company.

In this book, we have purposefully shied away from the term "MVP" (minimum viable product). The term was popularized by the Lean Startup movement, which played a major role in elevating the importance of running experiments. However, the term itself has become confused. Some take MVPs as an excuse not to have a clear vision and direction, which will never lead to a great business. Others treat MVPs as guidance to put out a crappy first version of a product, which doesn't teach you very much and can be self-defeating. We think these faults lie more in the interpretation than the theory, but regardless, we want to keep things simple. An experiment is a simple concept: it is a temporary process intended to test a hypothesis.

Even though the book begins with that wonderful quote from physicist Richard Feynman, what you won't find here is a religious application of the scientific method or statistical methodologies. Most startups simply do not have time to shoot for statistical significance. Furthermore, unlike science where there are immutable laws of nature, in business we deal with a far more irrational and unpredictable target: human beings. The experiments we talk about aren't driving towards incontrovertible truth. Instead, experiments inform better decisions.

This book is a small part of a larger canon on modern innovation and entrepreneurial techniques. For those interested in reading more, we've listed some of our favorite books and authors in the Appendix.

Experiments can feel challenging to run at first. People often start out with tests that are too complex, too long, or too product-centric. You'll find that things get easier and sharper with a bit of practice and the right mindset. We hope this book helps accelerate that process.

PART ONE

The Story

"There are no facts inside the building so get the heck outside."

STEVE BLANK
Entrepreneur and Author of *The Startup Owner's Manual*

IN WHICH DAS AND SIMON TEST THEIR ASSUMPTIONS
(And Discover a Bigger Business Opportunity)

Das and Simon were both engineers in the middle of their graduate degree programs. Six months before, they had a breakthrough in the lab. The two had invented a miniaturized gyro sensor that measured the speed, spin, and distance of a moving object with remarkable levels of accuracy. Das and Simon also happened to be fans of the most popular sport in the world: soccer.

When the two of them decided to take the leap into entrepreneurship, their project and their passion collided. They wanted to build a company that helped soccer players reach new levels of performance. Previously, it had been relatively easy to put sensors on the player, which could capture statistics like minutes played and miles ran. Das and Simon wanted to put their new sensors in the ball.

They were first-time entrepreneurs and wanted to do it right. They had researched the market size. They looked closely at the competition. Other approaches to measuring ball performance seemed clunky or inaccurate. The big sports brands like Adidas had some start-and-stop R&D efforts that were close, but nothing serious enough to scare them away. The two had also remembered the phrase "get out of the building!" from their entrepreneurship class, and started running customer discovery interviews with players and coaches.

Almost everyone they interviewed expressed interest in their idea. Both players and coaches were hungry for anything that could give them an edge. Who didn't want more performance data? When the two entrepreneurs pressed for any hesitations to buying their hypothetical ball, one fairly obvious fear came up again and again: how would it change the ball? Coach Emil Krewinsky, of the local university men's team, put it simply:

"Full stop, your ball has got to feel and play like a regular ball or no one's ever going to use it."

Still, Das and Simon were confident that they could finish the engineering work required to create a safe and commercially viable ball. With all this research under their belt, they were excited to move forward. Their plan was to get back into the lab and finish their product. Then they had their monthly check-in with their startup mentor Samantha.

Das gave Samantha the rundown. "We've spoken to 12 coaches and 37 players across the high school and university level. We were even able to speak to a professional player. We feel like we've validated the customer's goal. Put simply, players want to improve, and they are willing to spend money on gear that could lead to higher performance. There is hesitation over the safety and playability of the ball, but we think we can overcome that. Overall, what we've heard has been positive and pretty consistent. I'm not sure we'll learn anything new from more interviews right now. We feel like our next step is to get back into the lab, put in the work to finalize the product and pass initial safety tests, and then get a real product in people's hands."

Samantha nodded. "I can see why customers would be concerned about the ball. However, it sounds like you two think that will be more of a marketing challenge than a hard-core engineering one. During your interviews, did any other risks or questions about the business emerge?"

"The coaches were concerned about the kind of data they would get, and some wondered how we will get the data out of the ball," said Simon. "A few coaches want studies that prove how the data can lead to better performance. Das and I really do need to solve for getting the data out of the local memory in the ball. It should be straightforward, but there are three or four different engineering approaches we could take."

"When we add all this all up, it tells us that our big risk is getting the product right," said Das. "We need to go from prototype to working product, get the ball and the data in people's hands. We need to make sure that the ball passes final safety tests. We also need to ensure that the sensors can handle the pounding of consistent, ongoing usage. After that, we want to run a scientific study on the results people are getting with the new data. We've gotten three coaches to agree to a one-month study."

Samantha was quiet for a long minute.

"You might be right," she said. "You have done good work and have identified clear risks. And yes, when you start hearing the same things over and over again, that's not a bad time to slow down customer interviews until you have a new wave of questions to answer. That said, I would caution you not to rush back into the lab yet. A lot of startup teams get overly caught up with their product. They let engineering take precedence over validating the business."

"Well of course, we're engineers," laughed Das.

Samantha turned to her. "Let's say you solve the ball. It plays well and it's easy to access the data. Do you have other risks to consider?"

The two were stumped.

"Let's go back to basics. How would you describe your value proposition in a sentence?" asked Samantha.

Simon said, "We unlock your potential with a data-enabled soccer ball."

"Is your value really about the ball, or is that merely a means to get to the goal?" Samantha asked.

"I see where you are going," said Das. "How about this: we provide unique data through our sensor-enabled ball that leads to improved individual performance on the soccer field."

"Let's work with that. I see two big assumptions in that statement, how about you?"

"I guess the first assumption is that we can actually provide the unique data, and the second is that it will lead to improved performance," said Das.

"Yes. The first is all about solving your engineering challenges, but for the moment, let's assume that you do. The second, the improved performance for the player, still feels risky even if you solve your engineering challenges."

Samantha handed Simon and Das each some paper and a sharpie pen. "There are almost always creative ways to test a product's value proposition before you actually have the product. In your case, you have a hypothesis that players and coaches will find your new data extremely valuable for improving performance. How can you test that starting today? I want you to write down as many ideas as you can. Think about simple ideas and complex ones. Think about things that could take a day and things that could take a week or more. And think like a hacker, not an engineer. Your goal is to learn, not to create something robust. You have 5 minutes, starting now."

After five minutes, they reviewed the results:

1. Give players a close approximation of the data by setting up multiple camera angles at a practice game, and inputting coordinates and time frames into a physics simulation engine.

2. Adopt a team and act like consultants to the coach for a month, studying their play and suggesting areas of improvement.

3. Show a mock report to players and coaches and see what they say.

4. Put up a web page with a downloadable mock report, drive traffic to it with Facebook or Google ads, and see how many people ask us to make reports for them (maybe even for a price?).

5. Create a YouTube video that explains the ball, the sensors, and how the data can be used, and see if people ask for the product.

6. Run a Kickstarter campaign pre-selling the ball with a video that explains

its value proposition, and see if enough people contribute/buy.

"You might want to run several of these experiments, but let's pick one that feels relatively fast to get going yet will deliver believable information," said Samantha.

"The first two are very complex to pull off," Das said. "The landing page, number four, seems easy enough to do quickly, while a video could take some time. I also like the third, the idea of giving out a mock report, because we'll still be talking directly to potential customers."

"But will we be able to trust it?" said Simon. "I'm not sure that handing people just any old report will make them pay attention or take it seriously. They certainly won't be able to put someone else's data to work."

"What if you faked the ball?" said Samantha.

The two gave Samantha a confused look.

"There's a classic kind of experiment called a 'Wizard of Oz' test, where people think they are interacting with a real product, but in reality the startup team is doing everything manually behind the scenes. What if you told people that you were giving them your super ball, but actually just gave them a regular old soccer ball? Could you pull off reasonable approximations of real, personalized reports, even with players using a normal ball?"

"The reports would be pretty hacky," said Simon. "But yeah, if we didn't have to give them the reports on the spot, we could videotape a practice, focus on a small handful of players, and then approximate something that wasn't crazy. It'll be wrong, and you know how engineers hate wrong, but it won't be crazy wrong."

"That would lead to more believable reactions compared to giving people a random report," said Das. "We could probably pull it off with one soccer team to start. I've actually got one in mind."

"While you will want to run this experiment on more than one team, it's actually really smart to start with just one," said Samantha. "Think of it like a trial run to work out the kinks of the experiment and to figure out how labor intensive it really is. After the first one, I would encourage you to squeeze in as many as you can into a two week period. But first let me ask you, what needs to happen for you to consider the experiment a success?"

"How about if they ask to keep the ball? Or ask for more reports? Although if I'm honest, what I really want to know is whether they can put the data into practice and make themselves better," said Simon. "Could we measure that?"

"Isn't the ultimate test of whether they value the data going to be if they buy the ball?" said Das. "What if we took pre-orders?"

"I guess that would have the added benefit of seeing how people make a purchase decision," said Simon.

Samantha gave the two an experiment template to fill out, and by the end, they had the following:

What hypotheses do we want to prove / disprove?
We believe that players will find our reports valuable enough to pre-order the ball at best, and at minimum ask for more reports.

For each hypothesis, what is our pass/fail metric?
30% of players in the experiment pre-order the ball

75% of players ask for more reports

Who are the participants of this experiment?
High school and college soccer team players; we should focus on forwards (strikers) and midfielders first because they will care most about ball pace and spin.

How many do we need?
Three players per team

Three high school teams and one college team

How are we going to get them?

We'll go through the coaches. We have already spoken to the coaches of several teams during our customer discovery work and think they will agree.

How do we run the experiment?

One of us will attend a practice game or competitive game and take video. We'll analyze the video and come up with approximations of the sensor results. The next day, we will give the players and their coach the reports.

How long does the experiment run?

We'll run the total experiment for 2 weeks, after the initial trial run. With each team, we'll give the players a week from the live game to see if they want to pre-order the ball.

Are there other qualitative things we want to learn during this experiment?

What data in the reports is most interesting to them?

What data is most confusing to them?

What kinds of things are they hoping to improve the most with the data?

Who is more interested, the player or the coach?

How have they tried to put the data into practice (i.e. how did they try to improve) and what happened?

Armed with their next step, the two hopeful entrepreneurs thanked Samantha and left to start putting the plan into action.

INITIAL CURVE BALLS

Das immediately gave Coach Henderson, of the local high school boys team, a call. She had met him once during their customer discovery interviews, and thought that he would be open to helping further. She pitched him on using their ball in their next practice game.

"I'm just not willing to let my players use a prototype ball that hasn't been vetted for safety," he said. "I can't risk head injuries with my kids."

Das, thinking quickly, replied, "I can promise that the ball will feel and play just like a normal ball. One of our advisors is Coach Smith with the women's team at Hinckville College — if she vouches for the ball, would you be willing to give it a try?"

"Sarah Smith? I've heard of her. Okay, have her give me a call. I won't use the ball in a real game but a practice would be fine. I'm interested to see what this thing spits out and if it can help my boys."

Das let Coach Smith know the secret behind the experiment, and she and Simon soon found themselves recording a practice game. They spent a late night trying to study the footage and piece together reasonable reports.

"I think we can put something together for two of the three forwards that played, but I'm doubtful on the third," said Simon. "The footage isn't good enough. I don't think we can do the midfielders or we'll be up all night."

The next day, they dropped off the two complete reports at the coach's office and scheduled a follow-up conversation for a few days later. Afterwards, they assessed how the first part of their experiment went.

"Well, Coach Henderson was certainly willing to give this a shot, although it was interesting that he only wanted printed copies. I guess we need to remember that the coaches might not be very technically savvy. It's a shame that we could only get two reports done. Next time the two of us should simultaneously record video from opposite sides of the field. We should probably still stick to three players per team. If last night was any indication, even that many will take us five or six hours of analysis. If we do that, I think we might be able to work with two additional teams during this two week period."

"Well, I had an idea about that," said Das. "I was thinking about coding up a little utility application that would spit out estimates a lot faster, just so we're not having to do everything completely by hand. If I clear my plate and dedicate tomorrow to it, I think we could involve four or five teams, rather than two. Let's divide and conquer. You recruit as many teams as you can within a two-hours drive, and I'll get cracking."

Two days later, Das had hacked her tool together. Simon had recruited 2 other teams and was still playing phone tag with four others. They went back in to meet Coach Henderson. He waved the printed reports at them.

"I took a quick look at these the other day," said the coach, "But I'm not really sure what to do with them. There's a lot of numbers on here. This row shows me estimated speed of the ball during passes and during shots on goal, right? And this is spin? What do I do with it? What is good or bad?"

"Would it be useful to compare your results against some of the college players? We've also been studying their results," said Simon.

"I guess I'll know it when I see it," said the coach. "But it might be more useful than this."

"Okay, we'll get that to you tomorrow," said Simon. "Can I ask what the two strikers thought of the data?"

"The kids? I haven't given the reports to them," said the coach. "Not sure they'll be able to make sense of it either."

When Das and Simon left the coach's office, they were a little down.

"He wasn't as excited as I was hoping," said Das. "He was more confused than anything and ignored much of the data on the report. But I guess it does make sense that he needs some benchmarking data. I'll try to come up with something. And next time we should give the coach extra copies of each report and explicitly ask them to share with the players."

"Yeah. We're going to need to talk directly to the players if we're going to test whether they would pre-order our ball. I should have asked permission for that before we got started. Good thing we ran one of these before doing the rest."

THREE WEEKS LATER

Das and Simon sat down with Samantha once again. "How did it go?" their mentor asked.

"Complicated," said Simon.

"Yes, both depressing and exciting at the same time," said Das. "Simon did a great job recruiting four teams. The whole thing took us over three weeks, not two. It took a bit of convincing to be able to interact directly with the players, not just the coaches, but we got there in the end. But we didn't get any pre-orders at all. Not one. They didn't really know what to do with the data, even when we gave them benchmarking comparisons against similar players as well as more advanced players."

"There was one area where everyone seemed to be most interested, and that was set pieces. Set pieces are things like free kicks and corner kicks. Spin, speed, and arc are really important for set-piece kicks. Ever hear of the movie Bend It Like Beckham? Everyone wants to be Beckham. They want that fancy curl," said Simon. "But Das and I aren't interested in creating a ball just to practice set pieces. Some kind of market might be there but it feels a lot smaller."

"This experiment has made us realize two things," said Das. "The first is that our fantasies of an overnight success are unlikely. The data our ball collects is only interesting to a subset of players, and even with them, there is a lot of market education to be done before they know what to do with it. However, we've realized that perhaps we've been so fixated on the ball that we missed a bigger market opportunity. Neither players nor coaches at the amateur level have an effective, structured way to analyze trends."

"Trends?" asked Samantha.

"I mean tracking and reporting on how someone is performing over time. The pro teams have big budgets for this. They track tons of data both on and off the field. They obsess over their statistics. All of that is really uncommon at the college and high school level because of both complexity and cost. Maybe that is what we should be solving — taking some of what the pros do and making it accessible to the amateur team level. Honestly, this could be so much bigger than our soccer ball. It could be useful for many sports and many kinds of sensor devices. We could get going without having our ball at all. Instead it might be better to focus on integrating and analyzing data from the many other wearables that are out there, like Fitbit and STATSports."

"I think we need to do a bit more research in what the pro teams are doing, but it's an exciting direction," said Simon. "We have some thinking to do about whether we make our own devices at all. In some ways, it's like we are back at square one, but we know so much more now. Without the customer discovery and experiments, we might have wasted months and completely missed a bigger opportunity staring us in the face."

Samantha sat back. "I have to say that I'm impressed with both your experiment and your thought process. You really threw yourself into it and you were fearless about interacting with customers and being honest about your ideas. It's a shame that your results were not stronger, but you're wiser for it. Your shift in strategy sounds interesting, but you know what I'm going to say."

"Run an experiment!" the two said with laughter.

Lessons Learned

So what are the key takeaways from Das and Simon's adventure?

1. You learn a ton when you put people through an experience and watch their behavior and decisions.

2. It's really easy for creators to obsess about their product, but you need to think about your business risks beyond the product itself.

3. There is almost always a way to test your value proposition before you've finished the product itself. You'll usually be surprised by something important.

4. You don't have time to run experiments on everything. Test the most important risks and assumptions.

5. For any single assumption, there are always many different experiments you could run. Choose the one(s) that will give you believable information in a practical amount of time.

6. Create a structured plan for your experiment before you start. A chaotic experiment leads to chaotic results.

7. It's best to set your experiment's success (and failure) metrics before you begin, with hard numbers, even if they are based on guesses. Otherwise it's too easy to rationalize your results after the fact.

8. Do a trial run for any important experiment. You'll usually discover important adjustments to make that will improve your efficiency and ability to trust your findings.

9. Weave customer interviews into your bigger experiments in

order to maximize learning and insights.

10. Keep an open mind about your results, good or bad, and use your judgement when interpreting what you learn.

11. An external, objective opinion can be very helpful. Find a good mentor like Samantha! (see the Appendix for tips)

PART TWO

The Why & The How

"Time is really the only capital that any human being has, and the only thing he can't afford to lose."

THOMAS EDISON

Why We Run (and Don't Run) Experiments

"The only way to win is to learn faster than anyone else."
ERIC RIES
Author of *The Lean Startup* and
The Startup Way

We run experiments in order to make better decisions. We don't run experiments for their own sake. Put another way, we run them to gather crucial information that helps us formulate better strategies and take smarter actions in less time and with less cost.

It's the "less time and cost" that particularly confuses people, because they think that experiments add time and cost. Oddly enough, we all understand and accept the phrase "measure twice, cut once." We don't question it when it's a carpenter, because we recognize that the time taken for that second measure is a minuscule cost compared to the huge waste of getting something fundamental wrong.

For innovators, experiments are that "second measure." But boy, do our brains hate them. Most people have a psychological bias where we avoid a guaranteed cost in front of us if the gain (or avoidance of an even bigger cost) in the future is uncertain. We don't want to lose the time when it might have been unnecessary. "We're under the gun to ship this, so we simply don't have time!" runs the common refrain.

That's not all. Entrepreneurship (and innovation of any kind) takes confidence, conviction, creativity, determination, and perseverance. All of these are important strengths but they can also be treacherous. We fool ourselves into over-confidence in our ideas because we get lost in a fantasy of future success, or we're secretly scared of being wrong, or not-so-secretly scared of being beaten by someone else. We refuse to even contemplate failure, so we try to bull our way through with pace and effort and determination. We avoid facing the hard truths. With some people, it really does take being burned by their own hubris before they allow the time to ask tough questions about the big, uncertain things. Innovation has a tendency to humble its participants. Even Steve Jobs had the Lisa and NeXT. Even Jeff Bezos had the Amazon Fire.

The answer is not to avoid grand visions. The answer is to reality-check yourself and your execution plans. That's not being weak. That's being smart. If you believe that people will behave in a certain way, go test it now, not months from now after you've invested a lot of time and money. We guarantee that even if you end up being right (we hope so!), your experiment will not be a waste of time. You will learn nuances about your customers' behaviors, preferences and priorities that would be impossible to get when you're locked in your own head or in a room with your team. The results will inform your execution plans in ways that only make you better and more successful.

To do this, you need to learn how to do a few things:

1. Prioritize risks so that you only run experiments on things that matter

2. Design and run effective, compact experiments that deliver insights

3. Structure a decision-making process that helps you move fast
    with inevitably imperfect information

    Let's get to it.

Starting with First Principles

"The first principle is that you must not fool yourself — and you are the easiest person to fool."

RICHARD FEYNMAN
Physicist

Before you dive into either interviewing customers or running experiments, you need to take a step back and figure out what you need to learn and whom you need to learn it from. First, you should define the key choices and assumptions behind your intended business model. Second, you'll want to identify and prioritize the risks inherent in those assumptions.

Behind every new idea is a vision for how the world could and should work. Underpinning that vision is a stack of assumptions and beliefs. For example, here are some of Das and Simon's core assumptions when they started their journey:

- They believed that soccer players and coaches were always looking for new ways to improve performance.
- They believed that soccer players could benefit specifically from their sensor data.

- They believed that high school and college coaches would be a marketing channel and players would be their paying customers.
- They believed that they would make money by selling the ball and would do so through traditional retail partners.

You will have your own stack of assumptions and beliefs. When you start, some can correctly be called facts, but most will be educated guesses. If you're a subject matter expert, that can be hard to acknowledge. We've seen many people with twenty-plus years of experience in an industry maintain unyielding conviction in their opinions and plans, only to have the market knock them back down to size the hard way. This wasn't because they got their vision wrong, but because they got the details wrong. Let's face it — building something new is an exercise in predicting the future, and people are not very good at predicting the future. This is a truth lurking behind even the most glossy of startup success stories. Accepting that fact is as liberating as it can be unnerving.

There are a number of different frameworks that you can use to help shake out your assumptions. Many use Alex Osterwalder's business model canvas. I like to use the assumptions exercise from *Talking to Humans*. You can also look at Ash Maurya's lean canvas and David Bland's assumptions mapping exercise. We recommend that you try out more than one, and choose the one that you like best. None take that long to complete if you've already thought deeply about your business concept.

If we boil it down to basics, all of these frameworks are trying to unearth answers to very simple questions around your idea:

- Who is this for?
- What problem or need are we solving for them?
- How will we solve it?
- How will we acquire and retain our customers?
- How will we create value for our company? (This could be

monetary or non-monetary)

- How could it go wrong?

That last question can be the most useful for teasing out risks. Phrased in a slightly more formal way, it reads: "What assumptions do we have that, if proven wrong, could cause our business to fail?"

Once you have laid out your assumptions and risks, you need to prioritize them for the items that have the highest potential impact and the greatest uncertainty. In other words, which are the really scary ones? If you're a visual thinker, you can use sticky notes and a simple 2x2 matrix to plot them out.

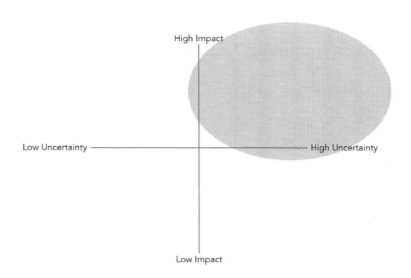

Items in the top-right quadrant are your risky assumptions. This is where you focus your research and experiments.

Why is this matrix useful? It's because you, the reader, live in the real world. You have real time pressures. You have to make decisions, you have to execute, and you simply can't test everything. If your company is like most, you will probably feel a lot of pressure not to test anything at all, but that's a mistake. Since you need to spend your time wisely, you obviously want to prioritize experiments for risk that are important and potentially costly if you are wrong. For the items in the top right quadrant, you will still end up using your judgment regarding which ones to test first. If you are undecided on which risk to start with, choose the one that you can test the fastest. We usually encourage teams to start with a few smaller, faster experiments that get them learning from the market immediately.

NOT JUST FOR STARTUPS

Experiments are just as powerful for proven, existing business as they are for startups. You don't need to ask the deeply existential questions, but you still need to examine your risks. This is true for a new product feature, a major pricing change, a new marketing initiative, etc. In these situations, the frameworks referenced above will feel like overkill. However, you still want to take a step back and ask similar questions: Who is this for? What are we predicting they will do? What value will they get? What value will we get? What could cause this [feature/initiative/change] to fail to deliver value to either our customers or our business? From those basic answers, you can figure out what you need to learn before you commit to spending a lot of time and money.

EXPOSING RISKS THROUGH A FINANCIAL MODEL

Another invaluable way to expose both assumptions and risks is through a lightweight financial model. You don't need to be an accountant or MBA to do this. It's really just another design challenge. Mark Suster, former entrepreneur and now venture capitalist, once wrote, "Your financial model tells a story." A lot of product-oriented entrepreneurs hate dealing with spreadsheets, but if you're going to be an entrepreneur, you need to understand your own story. You need to expose the critical guesses underpinning your story. Few things do that better than a blank spreadsheet needing to be filled out.

To keep things simple, create a monthly model that goes out 24 months after you first start accepting users or customers. Model some basic numbers for:

- How many customers you get each month, by what means and with what cost
- How many customers pay you and how much do they spend
- How many customers stick around and for how long
- How much it costs to fulfill each customer
- How much it costs to run the business with your desired investments and estimated customer growth

You might counter that this model will be fantasy, and you would be right. No model survives contact with the market. Do this exercise anyway. The goal here isn't to create a solid financial forecast. The point is to expose key assumptions, unknowns, and business pressure points. We guarantee that if you do this thoughtfully, you will expose some key inputs where you really don't know the answer. You can plug in educated guesses by doing your research and talking to people with relevant experience (investors, other entrepreneurs, and subject-matter experts), but you're often going to want to test, and thus inform, those key levers with experiments.

We strongly encourage you to do this exercise by starting with an empty spreadsheet rather than a pre-built model. If you do the latter, you will be working with someone else's assumptions on how your business works, rather than developing your own.

What Makes a Good Experiment?

"Requirements are actually hypotheses... realizing this should be liberating."

DAVID BLAND
Innovation Coach and Author

Once you know what you want to test, you need to figure out how to test it. The possibilities are endless, but all good experiments share five core traits:

1. They are **structured** and planned. You don't wing it and just start throwing things against the wall. Example: Das and Simon used an experiment template to lay out the components of their experiment (we'll cover the template in detail next).

2. They are **focused**, testing a core hypothesis and not trying to do too many things at the same time. Example: Das and Simon chose to test whether players would pre-order their ball.

3. They are **believable**, meaning that you have designed them in such a way that you can generally trust what you are learning, even if you have to use your judgment to interpret the results. Example: Das and Simon discarded the idea of paper-testing reports that weren't personalized to a player. Instead, they ran

an experiment where the participants believed that the data was real.

4. They are **flexible**, meaning that the team running the experiment is open to making small improvements as you go, without introducing so many new variables that you can't make sense of the data coming in. Example: Das and Simon did a trial run, and adjusted their approach to not only make the experiment easier to run but also to increase the quality of the information coming back.

5. They are **compact**, meaning that you can run them in an efficient amount of time. You don't want to get lost building and running an experiment. That would defeat the entire purpose of faster, more informed decision making. Example: Das and Simon time-boxed their experiment to two weeks and pushed hard to move fast, even though they ended up needing an extra week.

When it comes to actual tactics, you are only limited by your creativity and the desire to be constrained by those five traits. Here are a few common experiment archetypes, which we'll analyze in much more detail later on in the book:

- **Landing Page**: where you create a simple web page (or website) that expresses your value proposition and gives the visitor the ability to express their interest with some sort of call to action.
- **Advertising**: advertising your value proposition to a relevant audience to see whether people respond.
- **Promotional Material**: a variation of an advertising test where you produce some sort of online or offline promotional material to test reactions or generate demand.
- **Pre-selling** (including crowd-funding): where you try to book orders before you have built the product.
- **Paper Testing**: applying primarily to software and information (data, analysis, media, etc) products, paper tests are where you

mock up an example of an application user interface or report and put them in front of a potential customer.

- **Product Prototype**: a working version of your product or experience that is built for learning and fast iteration, rather than for robustness or scale.

- **Wizard of Oz**: where the customer thinks they are interfacing with a real product (or feature), but where your team provides the service in a manual way, hidden behind the scenes (hence the name).

- **Concierge**: where you manually, and overtly, act as the product you eventually want to build (unlike a Wizard of Oz where people are behind the scenes).

- **Pilots**: where you put an early version of your product in the hands of your customers, but you scale down the size of the implementation and put a finite time period on the project.

- **Usability**: where you check to see if someone can effectively use a product without getting stuck or blocked.

CREATING AN EXPERIMENT ROADMAP

Experimentation is an ongoing process, not a point-in-time exercise. To reinforce this concept, it can be very useful to create a loose roadmap for your risks and experiments. A risks roadmap plots out the risky assumptions to the business and ranks the order you want to address them. A corresponding experiments roadmap lists out the order of planned activities. Think of these as sketches, and don't get lost in planning. These are living documents that will change rapidly as you learn from the market.

As you think about prioritization, you'll usually want to start with quicker and easier ideas. For example, if testing your riskiest assumption requires you to build your product, then that would not be the first thing to do. We've found that there tends to be a natural progression where you begin with customer discovery interviews and smaller, tactical experiments, and then move into larger, more experiential tests like Wizard of Oz and Concierge experiments.

As you think about speed and progression of learning, it's worth considering a simple visualization that we call the Truth Curve.

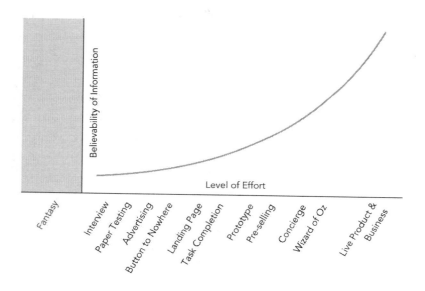

Put simply, the level of effort behind an experiment correlates to the believability of the information that emerges from it. You will always need judgment to interpret results, however the further left you are on the chart, the more judgment is required. Furthest left is qualitative research (i.e. talking to people) which is easy to do and incredibly powerful, but ranks relatively low on the "believability" scale because often what people say they are going to do is not what they do in practice. That doesn't mean you should skip over interviews. They provide essential insight, and there is an art to doing them well, as we cover in the prequel *Talking to Humans*.

Full "truth" exists at the far right when you have a live product in the marketplace. With a live product in market, you can measure hard results about whether are people using your product, buying it, referring it, and staying with it. You can see exactly how your profit and loss economics are working (or not working). You just don't want to wait until that point to start gathering insights and validation, because by then you might be out of both money and time.

The Anatomy of an Experiment

"In preparing for battle I have always found that plans are useless, but planning is indispensable."

DWIGHT EISENHOWER

If you have prioritized what you want to learn and have chosen where you want to start, you now need a plan. A well-run experiment requires discipline. Casual, chaotic experiments lead to chaotic data. Chaotic data is hard to analyze, trust, or use to inform decisions. We recommend using a template to structure your thinking. The simplest version of this is a single sentence: For [customer segment], we believe that [outcome] will happen when we run [experiment description].

However, we prefer a slightly more broken out version:

EXPERIMENT TEMPLATE

1. What hypotheses do we want to prove / disprove?
2. For each hypothesis, what quantifiable result indicates success? i.e. your pass/fail metric(s)

3. Who are the target participants of this experiment?
4. How many participants do we need?
5. How are we going to get them?
6. How do we run the experiment?
7. How long does the experiment run for?
8. Are there other qualitative things to learn during this experiment?

TEMPLATE EXPLANATION

Question 1: What hypotheses do we want to prove/disprove?

Every experiment needs a hypothesis statement. For example:

*   We believe that players will find our reports valuable enough to pre-order our soccer ball
*   We believe people will sign up to pay $5 a month for our product after visiting our landing page
*   We believe doctors in rural Zambia will have adequate (>0.5Mbps) mobile Internet access
*   We believe changing our product's on-boarding experience to have fewer steps will improve conversion rates

Smaller, tactical experiments should be tied to just one hypothesis. Larger, more experiential experiments, like the Wizard of Oz test Das and Simon ran in the story at the start of the book, may seek to investigate and validate more than one, but ideally no more than three, hypotheses. If you try to test too many things at the same time, you can dilute your focus, confuse the data coming in, and thus make it very hard to make decisions.

Question 2: For each hypothesis, what quantifiable result indicates success?

Every hypothesis should have a quantifiable pass/fail metric. For example:

- 30% (or better) of players in the experiment pre-order the ball
- 40% (or better) of participants will agree to pay $5 a month
- 70% (or better) of doctors in rural Zambia will have access to mobile Internet with >0.5Mbps
- We expect a 15% (or better) increase in conversion rates with the new on-boarding experience

Set your pass/fail goals ahead of time. If you don't, there is a strong risk that you'll find yourself rationalizing the acceptability of the results, whatever they are. If you are struggling to choose a metric, just take an educated guess. To get educated, research online for useful statistics and talk to people with relevant expertise. These people might be mentors, investors, other entrepreneurs, or a subject-matter expert. In every industry, you can find wise predecessors who have a sense of what "good" looks like.

Some teams freeze up at this point, fearing that the wrong number will deliver a false positive or false negative. We don't dismiss this concern, but if there is one underlying theme to this book, it is that you need to lean into uncertainty. Experiments in business are not like those in science. It is much harder, if not impossible, to control all the variables. Unless your product is already at massive scale, it is impractical to seek statistical significance. You also can't put total faith in previous data sets because people, business, cultures, and economies all change in unpredictable ways. In most cases, you are going to have to take an educated guess. That's okay. It is better to make an educated guess than to avoid setting any hard goals at all.

Sometimes your financial model, as discussed in the previous section, will help you set your pass/fail target. For example, let's say that you're counting on strong word of mouth to keep customer growth high and acquisition costs low. Your financial model reveals that you need at least 15% of your customers to invite at least 3 new customers. That is an experiment waiting to happen, and a ready-made metric to shoot for.

When in doubt, we believe in setting a high bar. We tend to be irrationally optimistic about our own ideas, and it is worth ruthlessly challenging them. Don't be afraid of high goals.

Question 3: Who are the participants of this experiment?

You might be amazed at how many teams dive into experiments without first considering whom they want to learn from. If you want to trust the results of your experiment, you must target the right people. Thus if you are working on a product for the elderly, don't run an experiment with all ages. If you are targeting business users, don't run your experiment with consumers. The more specific and narrow you can define this, the more confidence you'll have in the predictability of your results.

Most likely, you will also need to narrow your audience in order to make your experiment faster to start and practical to run. Products often need to handle many types of customers, which adds to their complexity and the scope of building them out, but experiments do not. Focusing the audience is a great shortcut to faster learning.

We're always asking, "How can we learn just as much with half the time and effort?" Often the answer to that comes in the form of restricting edge-cases or certain customer segments.

Question 4: How many participants do we need?

Set a target for how many people you want to recruit into your experiment. For enterprise/business products, you sometimes have to make do with low double digits. With a consumer product, you might want to engage hundreds or thousands of people. The exception is when you are testing for usability rather than value proposition. In that case, research has shown that single to double digits is usually adequate.

You need find a balance between involving enough participants that your data is believable, yet not so many that your experiment becomes impractical to run. You are not looking for incontrovertible proof. You are merely looking for a signal that can inform a better decision. Again, ask yourself, "How can we learn just as much with half the time and effort?"

If you can recruit enough relevant people, we recommend breaking up your experiment population into two or three groups. You'll often start an experiment and then realize that you want to make an adjustment. Sometimes this is because you made a mistake in the experiment design. Sometimes you spot an "aha!" insight that you want to investigate. Instead of running an experiment on everyone at the same time, running things in separate, phased cohorts creates the opportunity to iterate and evolve.

Question 5: How are we going to get them?

If you're going to run an experiment with people, you obviously need to go get them. The tactics you choose will totally depend on who you need and how many people you need. Here's a few examples of how we have recruited people in the past:

- Sending out personalized emails to people in our networks
- Researching prime targets and calling them directly on the phone
- Playing six degrees of separation and networking through relationships
- Attending relevant conferences or meetups, engaging with people, and asking for follow-up conversations
- Politely intercepting people before they walk into a store
- Approaching doctors in their lunch cafeteria
- Running online ads on Google, Facebook, Craigslist, etc.

(typically feeding those ads into a sign-up page or a short, qualifying survey so we could filter out the right kind of participants)

- Reaching out via existing email lists and newsletters
- Embedding our experiment into an existing product experience.

If you know the kind of people you need and how many you need, you should be able to work out how to get to them. This can feel intimidating to some people, but figuring out how to acquire customers needs to be a core capability for any team attempting a new venture. You need to learn how to do this through a combination of trial and error, looking for examples and inspiration online or offline, and mentorship. We share more recruiting tactics in the prequel *Talking to Humans*. Alternatively, you might bring someone onto your team who has a more natural bent towards sales, marketing or business development. When it comes to recruiting participants, it's important not to be passive nor to give up too quickly, without crossing over into being annoying. Be intrepid.

If you are planning on spending money to acquire participants, it's worth putting a budget limit in place, as well as checking that your budget is realistic for both the numbers you want to get and advertising platforms you plan to use.

Question 6: How do we run the experiment?

For this question, you want to list the high-level points describing the structure and execution of the experiment. For this question, you want to list the high-level points describing the structure and execution of the experiment. Your goal is not to exhaustively document every little detail of the plan, but to ensure that everyone has a shared understanding of the essentials. Writing this down in a shared document makes things crystal clear.

Question 7: How long does the experiment run?

Think through your context and goals. Some experiments can run for a day or a week. Others might run for a few months, especially for infrequent activities (although ask yourself if you can speed things up and still believe the information coming in). Keep on asking this refrain, "How can we learn just as much with half the time and effort?"

Question 8: Are there other qualitative things to learn during this experiment?

An experiment's primary goal is to put a hypothesis to the test. However, it also creates opportunities to talk directly to customers and glean further insights. This last question helps you structure these "ride-along" questions that often provide invaluable insights. If you want help thinking through the kinds of questions you should ask, and how to ask them, we would recommend that you read the prequel to this book, *Talking to Humans*, which is available for free at talkingtohumans.com.

A NOTE ABOUT TEAMS

One thing that isn't included in this template is the team itself needed to run the experiment. That will completely depend on the needs of the experiment and the resources you have available. However, in our experience, experiments tend to run better with cross-functional teams, usually with six people or fewer. You cannot always staff a team with an engineer, a designer, a product manager, and a marketer, but the more diversity you have across those skillsets, the better. Experiments will get designed and implemented better, and you'll have more perspectives to interpret results and spot insights. It's also beneficial to have a clear leader of the team. Having a final decision maker, even if everyone contributes to decisions, will help you move faster and not get lost in debate or doubt.

The Template in Practice

"You start a company on a vision; on a series of faith-based hypotheses. However, successfully executing a startup requires the company to become fact-based as soon as it can."

STEVE BLANK
Author of *The Startup Owner's Manual*

Let's now take that template and examine how it was used for a real experiment. We'll kick things off by sharing a story about why the experiment was run in the first place so that you understand the template in its full context.

A NEW REVENUE STREAM FOR COOKING LIGHT MAGAZINE

The team at *Cooking Light* magazine was under pressure. On the good side, they were the leading food magazine in the USA with two million print subscribers, another two million online readers, and an amazing library of tasty, dietician-approved recipes. But recipes had become commoditized online and advertising dollars were declining. They needed to find a new revenue stream. The editor-in-chief, Scott Mowbray, had an underlying insight: "Other than restaurants, the one thing people pay for in food is weight loss." The team believed that there was an underserved market of people who wanted to lose weight yet loved to cook, and initial editorial forays and customer interviews backed this up. The concept was to create a subscription business built on top of *Cooking Light's* amazing archive of test kitchen and dietician-approved recipes. They believed that consumers would pay for a daily meal planning service that delivered both a structured diet and great recipes. After doing initial research on the market and competitive landscape, the team jumped into the field to test those beliefs.

They had identified a set of risky assumptions, but the first thing they wanted to test was whether people would care about the concept. They ran a two-day experiment to test for demand. The first day was spent designing and building a web page (a landing page) that included the value proposition, the monthly price, and a simple form to sign up for a waiting list. The second day was spent driving traffic to the landing page through online ads, social media, and two email newsletters. This let the team test both the efficacy of those channels as well as get a peek into potential costs of acquisition.

The landing page tested three different monthly price points (called split-testing or A/B testing), and measured how many people signed up for the service. Conversion rates ranged from 11% to 20% across the different price points. These numbers were double the team's goal of 5% to 10%. The team was excited by those results, but also knew to take that data with a grain of salt since they didn't actually collect credit card information. However, they didn't stop there.

At this point, we get to the experiment that we'll use to demonstrate the template:

The team chose a dozen consumers from the waiting list and ran them through a Wizard of Oz product experience for two weeks. A Wizard of Oz test presents a real-looking product experience to the customer, but behind the scenes humans manually perform the necessary actions. In this case, the plan was to have Allison Lowery, the digital editor of *Cooking Light*, act as the algorithm and manually create meal plans for the participants, emailing those out every day. At the end of a two-week experience, the team planned to put a subscription price in front of participants and see how many would pay to continue. The team set a goal ahead of time that at least 50% of participants would agree to continue.

Before kicking off the Wizard of Oz, the team did an experiment about the experiment. They didn't know how many people Allison could support at one time, so they grabbed two colleagues from a separate team to be guinea pigs for a couple of days. From that trial run, the team learned that Allison could handle a dozen people with about a day's investment in automation (software code) cobbled together to help her.

From the landing page test, the team had a large waiting list of interested customers. They only wanted a dozen, but they didn't want to choose just any dozen. They wanted to select finalists who would minimize the complexity of the experiment, and that meant choosing people whose dietary preferences fit existing recipes. The team sent an email to a third of that waiting list, inviting them to fill out a survey that asked basic factual questions about family size and food requirements. From those responses, the team chose their 12 participants and proceeded to run the Wizard of Oz test. At the end of the two weeks, they told participants that it would be $15 a month to continue, and 11 out of 12 participants agreed to sign up.

The success of the Wizard of Oz test led the team to build out a financial model based on observed data and assumptions for customer acquisition and churn based on industry averages. Together, the positive results and financial promise induced Time Inc's then-CEO, Joe Ripp, to approve the funding needed to bring the product to market. As of the writing of the book, the business is still going strong at www.cookinglightdiet.com.

These experiments didn't just help the team test demand and justify investment. They also brought the team in direct contact with customers. By combining these experiments with interviews along the way, they gained valuable insights that steered the strategy and design of both the business model and the product.

Knowing this context, let's look at the template for the two-week Wizard of Oz experiment. In doing so, we'll cover both the template that fed into the experiment as well as the results.

TEMPLATE IN PRACTICE: COOKING LIGHT'S WIZARD OF OZ

1. What hypotheses do we want to prove / disprove?

We believe that consumers will pay for a meal-planning service utilizing our existing recipes.

2. For each hypothesis, what is our pass/fail metric?

50% or more participants will agree to pay $15 a month to continue the service.

Result: Success — 11 of 12 (92%) signed up.

Additional notes from participant interviews: Participants reported feeling pressured by receiving a new dinner recipe every night. We may want to introduce "leftover" nights. Participants also gave us feedback that the ingredients were expensive. We might need to adjust recipes that work well in a magazine context, which serves an aspirational purpose, to the more practical needs of a meal planning service.

3. Who are the participants of this experiment?

Consumers in the USA with 3 or 4-person families who are interested in losing or maintaining weight. To keep things simple, we will exclude consumers with large families, strict dietary restrictions, or food preferences that are either very narrow or do not fit our existing recipes.

Result: We were able to successfully run the experiment with these kinds of families.

4. How many participants do we need?

10 to 20 participants

Result: We decided on 12 participants after the initial trial run.

5. How are we going to get them?

We will send a survey (family size, dietary restrictions) to a third of the wait list created from our landing page test (200 people out of 600 on the wait list), and use that to narrow down participants.

Result: 60% of the 200 filled out the survey, leading to 71 qualifying potential participants. We picked the final dozen randomly from the 71.

6. How do we run the experiment?

We're going to run a Wizard of Oz test that fakes the product and tests conversion rate to paying customer. We'll onboard each participant with a phone call to discuss food preferences. Every day, the customer will get an attractive email that lists out their recommended breakfast, lunch, snack, and dinner. The dinner will be a Cooking Light recipe. After the first week, we'll interview the participants to see how they are doing. At the end of the second week, we'll explain that it will cost $15/month to continue and see how many sign up.

Allison will be acting as the "algorithm" creating the meal plans based on customer preferences. Before we begin the experiment, we will create an email template and hack together a recipe scraper that automatically pulls in ingredients and instructions into the email format.

Result: The experiment ran pretty well according to plan, with one exception. A day into the test, we learned that customers also wanted simple side dishes, and we had to quickly pull some together that paired well with our primary recipes.

7. How long does the experiment run?

Two weeks

Result: This ended up being enough time for someone to truly experience the planning service with their family, and cook our recipes for more than a couple days. We had more conviction in the results than if it had been one week.

8. Are there other qualitative things to learn during this experiment?

Why did people sign up for the trial?

Insight: While we thought a lot of people would be driven by weight-loss goals, a significant portion simply wanted an easier way to maintain a healthy lifestyle for themselves and their families.

Why did people agree to pay or not pay for the service?

Insights: Those who signed up told us they did so because they liked the combination of personalized recipes and the ease of having their meals already organized while not having to think about calories. The person who did not sign up did not cook enough of the recipes to make it worthwhile.

What did people think about the recipes?

Insights: On the whole, participants loved the recipes and gave us enthusiastic reports from their families. However, some found the ingredients a bit expensive. We were also missing simple side dishes. Our conclusion is that our library of recipes is indeed a powerful asset but we will need to make some adjustments for the broader market.

How often and when do people want to receive a meal plan (daily? weekly? both?)

Insights: People gave us feedback that they liked the daily emails, but requested a weekly summary ahead of time so they could shop on the weekend.

Will a shopping list be necessary?

Insights: The most requested feature was a shopping list which worked across the recipes for the week, and which also separated out the standard pantry staples (salt, olive oil) that customers likely already owned. We're not convinced that a shopping list needs to be in the earliest versions of the service, but we should design the print layout of the recipes with pantry staples clearly separated in order to make shopping easier.

Generating and Refining Experiment Ideas

"When we start off building a new feature or product, there are a million questions to answer. We have to find the answers to these questions before committing ourselves to building a solution."

MELISSA PERRI
Author of *The Build Trap*

My favorite way to design experiments borrows from a collaborative design exercise that some call a "design studio" and others call a "charrette". It is a rapid sketching exercise that helps people shed inhibitions and avoid over-thinking. It mixes both individual thought as well as group collaboration.

Total Time: 1 hour - 1.5 hours, depending on number of participants.

TOOLS

- Multiple 11x17" sheets of paper
- Fine Sharpie pens
- Masking tape dots, or another way to mount paper on the walls
- Experiment template

PREPARATION

Before you begin, you need to decide the risky assumption you want to tackle. This can be done ahead of time, or by dedicating 10 minutes to listing out the big risky assumptions in front of the team and then using the impact/uncertainty quadrant to force-rank that list.

The ideal team size is 4 to 8 people, so if you have a large group, break the team up into sub-groups.

Hand everyone a Sharpie and some 11x17" paper. Have everyone create a "six-up" by folding the paper in half along the short side, and then in thirds along the long side. You end up with six boxes on each piece of paper.

Make sure everyone understands the chosen risky assumption. Explain the essentials of how the exercise will work and get going with the following steps.

STEP 1: SKETCHING (5 - 7 MINUTES)

Everyone is given 5 minutes to come up with as many different experiment ideas as they can think of that would help shed light on the big risky assumption. Using words and images, they should put a different experiment idea in each box on their page. For people who have never done this before, take a moment to explain that you are looking for any kind of activity that could help you understand if you are right or wrong about the chosen assumption.

Most people don't spend their days thinking like a hacker, but this is the time to do it. To jar people's thinking, you can provide the following prompts:

- What experiments might run in one day, or in one week, or in one month?
- What existing tools and services can be re-purposed for the

purposes of an experiment?

- Think about ideas that are boring and also ideas that seem slightly crazy.

Don't let anyone get bogged down on any one idea. Do be willing to give the team an extra minute or two if they need it, but don't tell them this ahead of time.

This isn't an art competition, and you will probably need to coach your team accordingly so that they don't tighten up. Here is a real example from one experiment design session:

As you can see, rough sketches are perfectly fine. Try to focus your team on the creative exercise and the communication of the ideas.

Tip: give people an extra sheet of paper to keep underneath the one they are drawing on to prevent the Sharpie from marking the table underneath. I love Sharpies because they loosen people up and are easy to see from a distance, but the ink does go through thin paper easily.

STEP 2: SHARING (10 - 30 MINUTES)

Going in turn, each person should put their paper(s) on the wall and concisely explain their concepts to the team. Don't let anyone present for longer than 2 or 3 minutes. During this sharing process, ask everyone to refrain from discussing what they think is a good versus bad experiment. Do, however, encourage the team to ask clarifying questions. You will likely need to actively moderate for this, but it is important. You will likely see the same concept come up more than once. When this happens, team members will often want to jump ahead when it is their turn to present. Encourage them to go through their concepts anyway, because you will often hear nuanced differences.

During this sharing process, ask everyone to individually note the experiments that sound most compelling. After 20 or 30 ideas, they can blur together, so it's worth recording the best concepts as you go along.

STEP 3: DOT VOTING (5 MINUTES)

Give everyone three votes for the concepts that they think are best. They can use the votes however they choose. To vote, just have each team member draw a dot (ideally with a pen of another color) next to the experiment they found compelling.

While this happening, mentally link up the ideas that are similar, so that you can combine their dots.

STEP 4: CHOOSE THE TOP IDEAS (2 MINUTES)

Select the top experiments, and in particular, select a number that is half the number of people doing the exercise (e.g. if you have 6 people, choose 3). The next step is to pair people up.

STEP 5: REFINE AND DEFINE (20 - 30 MINUTES)

Split the team into pairs and give each pair a different experiment idea. Each pair should refine the idea and fill out the components of the Experiment Template. As always, they should be asking themselves if the experiment can be made smaller and faster.

STEP 6: SHARE & DISCUSS (4-5 MINUTES PER PAIR)

Each pair should then present the details of their experiment. This time, the audience is allowed to provide suggestions and critique.

NEXT STEPS: ACTION

Hopefully this process has created a few experiments that you actually want to try. The point isn't to create sketches on paper. The point is to generate actionable data, so get to it! As you start implementing your chosen experiment(s), they will likely need further iteration, but this design studio is a great way to get things going.

CAUTION TAPE

Experiments are hard. They are hard to justify and hard to run. As you are designing your experiments, here are two of the biggest gotchas to be aware of:

AN EXPERIMENT IS NOT THROWING THINGS AGAINST THE WALL

We want to reiterate that the best experiments have structure rather than chaos. The worst experiments have multiple people running in multiple directions, trying different things at the same time. Every data point becomes a data point of one. The team is confused. Your learning is confused. This is a lazy way to run an experiment.

As a case in point, we recently worked with a startup that was exploring new pricing structures. Their first approach was to try several things at the same time. This confused the sales team (and thus likely confused prospects) and made it hard to interpret results. Instead, they switched to a process where they tested one pricing structure, observed and discussed the results across the team, and then evolved the structure based on what they had learned. It created calm and focus, allowed for better documentation of results, and fostered more thoughtful decision making.

Remember to work up from your building blocks. Your high-level vision should lead to identified assumptions and risks, which should lead to prioritized hypotheses to test. From those hypotheses, you should put an action plan in place and execute. Then you should review results and either draw conclusions or iterate your test. A good experiment has flexibility, but thoughtful flexibility. You should be willing to make changes if you feel like you can't trust the experiment, but not so many that the experiment loses all focus and structure.

DON'T OVER-BUILD

Lindsey Grey, a Partner at Two Sigma Ventures, has seen many startup teams run experiments and provided this warning: "Don't build too much — that is always failure mode. Teams get so invested in what they are making for the experiment that they lose sight that their creation is just to learn." You want to remember that an experiment should give you believable information, but it does not need to handle every customer and every situation. It is not meant to be permanent, scalable or re-usable. Your goal is to learn as much as possible, as fast as possible. Keep a hacker's mindset and think about the shortcuts that will dramatically speed things up.

Learning and Decisions
(a.k.a. the hard part)

"If we have data, let's look at data. If all we have are opinions, let's go with mine."

JIM BARKSDALE
former CEO of Netscape and AT&T WIreless

With practice, it gets easier to run good experiments. However, making critical, high-pressure decisions remains difficult. If you've made it this far, you've probably bought into the idea that experiments can help inform better judgment calls. We use the phrase "judgment calls" on purpose. Results are rarely clear cut. You will often get muddy data and mixed signals. You will have variables in the mix that pollute the purity of an experiment. You will always worry about false positives and false negatives. The members of your team will interpret the results differently. Startups and innovation teams don't operate in a controlled lab. Fighting against this is a waste of time, because of the speed at which new ventures need to operate.

Given all of this, how can you increase the odds of making good decisions?

GATHER GOOD DATA ON SOMETHING IMPORTANT

First, gather good data. If you are disciplined about choosing the big risks to tackle, and disciplined about designing and executing your experiments (which includes adjusting them mid-flight if needed), you will get much more believable, and ultimately actionable, data. Part of running a disciplined experiment is keeping the incoming data organized. Keep a running, consolidated source of key results. This can be a shared digital document or spreadsheet or a physical wall with sticky notes or a whiteboard. The method doesn't matter, just that you do it and do it in a way that gives the entire team easy access.

KNOW WHEN TO BE SKEPTICAL OF RESULTS

It's worth once again reminding ourselves of the Truth Curve:

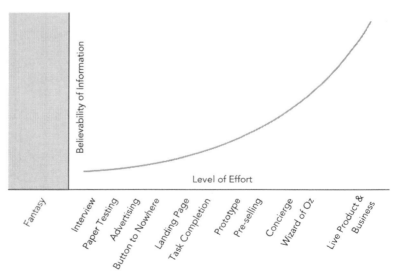

To reiterate the meaning of the chart, the level of effort behind an experiment correlates to the believability of the information that emerges from it. You will always need judgment to interpret results, however the further left you are on the chart, the more judgment is required. The tricky part is that our judgement gets poisoned by our own cognitive biases, which leads us to the next topic.

TRY TO AVOID YOUR OWN BIASES

Entrepreneurs are an irrationally optimistic lot. This is simultaneously a huge strength and weakness. It is really hard tamping down our excitement and hopes and even ego, but somehow we have to learn to ruthlessly reality check ourselves. Here is a list of common cognitive biases to keep guard against:

- Have you ever had a teammate who locked onto the first piece of data that came in and was ready to make a huge decision and race forward? "I just had the most amazing customer interview! We have to change everything!" That's **anchoring**: our tendency to fixate on one piece of information too heavily, often the first information that comes in.

- Have you ever felt the pull to highlight the data that proves your point of view, and dismiss or make excuses for the data that doesn't? Or you spent all your energy focusing on the people who liked your idea, and didn't spend enough time trying to understand the real root cause behind why others do not? That's **confirmation bias**: our tendency to prioritize and interpret information that supports our position, and filter out evidence that does not. This is hugely important to fight against, and why we set quantitative targets for experiments ahead of time so we can't rationalize our results after the fact.

- Have you ever felt yourself jumping to a conclusion or a point of view because it is popular? This is the **bandwagon effect**: our tendency to believe more in an idea if the people around us believe it.

- Have you ever felt the pain of killing a project after putting a lot of time, money, or personal capital into it? This is the **sunk cost**

fallacy: our tendency to resist changing or shutting down an initiative after investing in it.

If you've felt these forces working against you, you are not alone. You share these tendencies with the entire human race.

RUN A DISCIPLINED DECISION PROCESS

At the end of every experiment, you should be able to choose one of these four options:

1. You aren't satisfied and still need more data to make a key business decision
2. You are ready to move forward with the hypothesis with confidence
3. You decide to change your hypothesis based on the data (which might mean a new experiment)
4. You decide the kill the initiative entirely

Just because a single experiment fails, that doesn't mean you should kill your idea. And of course, just because an experiment succeeds doesn't mean you magically have product-market fit. As MIT professor Bill Aulet writes in his book *Disciplined Entpreneurship*, "In social science research, you do not prove hypotheses so much as disprove hypotheses, so a successful experiment only *suggests* a successful venture." (emphasis added)

If you are on a product team for an established company, you probably already have a way of making decisions. For ground-floor startups and innovation teams, we actually recommend the structure described next.

WEEKLY DECISION MEETINGS

If you are trying to aggressively vet an idea, you want to keep your feet to the fire. Weekly decision meetings are the best way to hold yourself and your team accountable to fast and sharp execution. The structure is quite simple:

1. Meet every week at a regularly scheduled time
2. Review what you hoped to learn and what you actually learned
3. Based on what you learned, make conscious decisions on both the experiments and the overall initiative itself. In other words, do you continue forward as-is, do you make changes, or do you kill the initiative?
4. Based on those decisions, what do you need to accomplish during the next week?

The attendees of the meeting should include the experiment team as well as any relevant "stakeholders". The latter is particularly important for anyone trying to run experiments in larger companies, which typically have more of a command-and-control type structure. Per the quote at the start of this chapter, in the absence of compelling new evidence, executives will go with their gut and existing data. If you involve key executives in the decision meeting, they become invested in what the team is trying to learn. They become hungry for more data to make a better decision, and they have a far greater likelihood of trusting what the team is learning.

To make this meeting run smoothly, it helps to have a member of the team synthesize what you have learned and document the key takeaways, data points and challenges. Sometimes a decision will have a clear consensus among the team, but not always. It's important to have a leader empowered to make the hard calls and drive things forward.

Lastly, the team should feel free to cancel the meeting if everyone is in the middle of a big experiment and there isn't enough new data to make decisions. However, too many cancelled meetings implies that the team is moving too slowly.

WATCH THE BIG PICTURE WITH RISK DASHBOARDS

If you are trying to de-risk a new business idea, you likely have multiple risky assumptions you are trying to evaluate and mitigate. We recommend using a risks dashboard to visualize the progress, or lack thereof, you are making. The image below is an example from the Cooking Light Diet story.

Risky Assumption	Status	Notes
The value proposition will resonate among people who like to cook		Conversion rates are strong, and we are seeing evidence of word of mouth
Our current recipes will work without additional investments		Clear feedback that ingredients are expensive, and we need side dishes
Consumers will accept the $15/month price point		Initial conversions are good but we need further churn/retention data
We can scale this beyond our current subscriber base		Initial experiments have been positive, but we haven't expanded real marketing yet
We can delay marketing investments by using parent co resources		Competition among projects is making us think we will need to rethink this strategy
Consumers will stay on our meal plan longer than most diets		We need another month of churn data to answer this
Our brand should be positioned in lifestyle category, not diet		Untested

Original dashboard design by Nicole Rufuku and Amanda Lasnik

As you can see in the image, the dashboard lists out important risky assumptions, includes a color code, and then a concise status report.

The colors are quite simple:

- Grey if no experiments has started yet
- Green (+) if results are coming back positive (light green for weak confidence, dark green for strong confidence)
- Red (-) if results are coming back negative (light red for weak confidence, dark red for strong confidence)

This dashboard isn't meant to document every assumption and experiment. Focus on the high-impact assumptions and keep it at a high level. Think of it as a running snapshot of your confidence, as well as a way to hold yourself accountable to facing the big risks (you don't want a lot of grey "untested" spheres on the board).

You'll want to review it on a weekly basis in your decision meetings, and treat it like a living document. You might find yourself swapping out some of the risky assumptions as your point of view evolves, but just be careful not to do that in an attempt to hide the red (negative) results.

PAY ATTENTION TO OUTLIERS

Sometimes your outliers and edge cases are the source of the biggest insights. As you are trying to interpret the results of your experiments, it's important not to dismiss these data points too quickly. Here's a case in point:

Steve Blank once shared a story of a startup team building an enterprise software product. They tested a pricing model of $9.99 per month/per user with 50 different companies. They received a strong, positive signal from 47 of them. When Steve asked about the three outliers, the team explained that those three also wanted to buy, but instead wanted an enterprise license for $10,000 a year. The team had been so focused on their success metric of 47 out of 50 participants that they hadn't fully examined the implications of those three edge cases. You've probably already figured it out: if the startup team was expecting to sell thousands of seats per account, then a $10K site license would be a terrible idea. However, if they were only selling a handful of seats, then those three edge cases might just have given them a huge clue as to how to charge significantly more.

THE BIG DECISIONS

We wish we could tell you when to kill an idea and when to commit, or how to choose one path over the other, but any advice we would give would be irresponsible. If there is one fact we've learned over decades dealing with startups is that every single one has its own context. The same thing applies to innovation and product teams. It's wise to learn from previous successes and failures but ultimately you have to make decisions within your context. That means your market, your market timing, your product, your business model, your company's own strengths and weaknesses, and more. Getting too prescriptive, or trying to copy someone else's playbook too closely, is a recipe for failure.

The pressure is on you (or your designated leader) to make the big calls. In the process, you'll need to be decisive and timely with your decisions. As a leader, you can only hope to get more right than wrong. Just remember that you are not on your own. With that statement, we're not just referring to your mentors, bosses, or teammates. We're also talking about your market. By listening, observing, and experimenting, you'll uncover a tremendous amount of information that will set you on a smarter path. Don't abdicate your vision to your customer, nor take customer requests too literally, but do find that balance between judgment and data.

We strongly believe that the best decisions come from a mix of judgment and data. When people swing too far to one side or the other, they tend to go wrong. Both intuition and data, even large quantities of it, can be deceiving, but together they give you an edge.

Throughout all of this, keep in mind that we don't run experiments for their own sake. We run them to formulate better strategies and take smarter actions in less time and with less cost.

PART THREE

Important Considerations

"Kick-start your brain. New ideas come from watching something, talking to people, experimenting, asking questions and getting out of the office!"

STEVE JOBS

Testing the Business vs Testing the Product

"Starting with a solution is like building a key without knowing what door it can open."

ASH MAURYA
Author of *Running Lean* and *Scaling Lean*

A few years ago, we met an entrepreneur who had created an amazing new device and corresponding service for telemedicine. He was running creative experiments for his startup, but they were all centered around the efficacy of his product. It was perfectly rational that he wanted to prove that his product worked and delivered value. The problem was that he wasn't testing his revenue model at all, which is both complex and critical in healthcare. He had a dozen possible ways he could have packaged, priced, and distributed his product, some of which could have unlocked his business and some of which could have created tremendous friction. He wasn't putting in the time to figure out which was which.

When we mentor new startup teams, we see this problem over and over again. The question "Will people find my product valuable and desirable?" is really important, but it's not enough. As a matter of fact, after nearly a decade in the "lean startup" community, we've come to believe that customer acquisition, channel, and revenue model changes (or "pivots") tend to have the biggest impact on a startup's trajectory.

Let's look at another version of how our story with Das and Simon, and their data-collecting soccer ball, might have played out.

IN WHICH DAS AND SIMON EXAMINE THEIR BUSINESS MODEL

"I know you two are eager to work on your prototype," said their mentor Samantha, "But I really think you need to put a little more focus on de-risking your actual business beyond the product itself. Let's start someplace simple: how are you planning on making money?" Samantha asked.

"Once the ball is finished, we were just planning on selling it through Amazon's marketplace and the big sports retailers like Dick's Sporting Goods," said Simon. "We might set up our own e-commerce site for direct orders, but we figured we should go where the customers are. I would think the retailers will be excited about something techie at a higher price point."

"You might be right," said Samantha, "But I would challenge you to stretch your thinking. How you choose to make money and how you choose to acquire your customers will make a big difference to your success or failure. Let's take your revenue model. You could charge for the ball and try to make a nice profit on each unit. On the flip side, you could sell it at cost, or even give it away for free, and make your money by hosting the data or by selling tools that access and analyze the data."

"That's true. We hadn't really thought about creating a subscription business like that," said Das.

"It might be a smart idea or an idiotic one. I can't tell you what is good or bad, but I do know that you two should think more about this," said Samantha. "You need to develop a strong point of view on who you will sell to, how you will market and sell them, and how you will actually make money. On top of that, your choices of target customer, customer acquisition method, and revenue model must all fit together. I know you two think of yourselves as engineers and not business people, but this is imperative to spend time on. I promise, you are more business savvy than you think."

"We've thought a little bit about this but probably not enough," said Das. "For our target customer, we believe that we should start at the high school or college level, not professional teams, but we haven't decided which. We also haven't decided whether we should aim at coaches or players. We were thinking about players because, as Simon said, we figured we would sell through retailers. We're hoping to get coaches to recommend the ball, but have players actually go buy it."

"I'm hearing a bunch of assumptions tucked in there. It might be useful for you to map out your problem space and then run additional market research and some focused experiments," said Samantha. She went up to her whiteboard and wrote out the following options:

Target Customer	Sales Channel	Revenue Model
Player	Sell direct - online	Sell the ball
Coach	Sell direct - sales force	Sell software
Parent	Retail partners - online	Sell data
	Retail partners - stores	Sell data storage
High School	Distributor (wholesaler)	Sell advertisements
College	OEM to sports brands	
Adult/Club		
Professional		

"What does OEM mean?" asked Simon.

"That stands for original equipment manufacturer. If you were an OEM, you would make the ball, but strike a partnership with an established company like Adidas to sell it under their brand and through their channels."

"Whoa," said Simon. "That never occurred to us."

"You've been doing some good interviews with coaches and players, but I really would recommend that you talk to a few industry experts from the sports equipment world, either on the retail or manufacturing side," said Samantha. "I bet that you would learn a ton about different models, the market power of different players, and the pros and cons of various approaches. Even if you decide to break from convention, it's best to be informed about what has worked and failed in the past. However, I also think that you can accelerate your learning by developing a hypothesis here and testing it."

She pulled out some sticky notepads and sharpie pens. "Knowing your options is a good thing, but you can't test a menu. You need to test something specific. For this next exercise, I want you to think about those variables on the whiteboard, or any new ones I missed, and come up with combinations that feel interesting and viable. Write them down — one per sticky note. I'll give you three minutes."

By the time three minutes had passed, the two had created the following list:

1. Sell the ball to players through retailers, targeting high school and college

2. Sell the ball to high school+college players through an online store, targeting high school and college

3. Sell the ball through a major brand as an OEM, letting the brand drive customer targeting

4. Sell the ball to college coaches through a direct sales force

5. Give the ball away (or sell at cost?) and charge college coaches a subscription fee to host data in the cloud

6. Directly sell the ball at cost (or free?) to college coaches, and up-sell a software tool that extracts and analyzes the data

7. Sell the ball at cost through retailers and up-sell a benchmarking tool (and data) to purchasers, targeting high school and college

"If you had to choose at most two things from that list to explore, what would you choose?" asked Samantha.

The two conferred and Das replied, "We still want to test selling through the retailers, but we also think it is worth exploring some variation of #5 and #6 where we sell some kind of subscription to coaches as our real money-maker."

"Let's start with the first," said Samantha. "You believe that you can successfully sell your ball directly to players through retailers. What assumptions do you have behind that statement that, if proven wrong, would cause it to fail?" She pointed to their sticky notepads again, and in another three minutes they had the following list.

Hypothesis: we can successfully sell the ball to players through retailers
Risky assumptions:

1. Retailers want to carry our product

2. Retailers will deal directly with us rather than insist on a wholesaler

3. We can generate enough consumer demand even if we do get the ball into retail stores

4. Consumers will buy our ball without needing a sales person trained on our value prop

5. Our return rates will be low

6. We can be profitable at a price that consumers like and with the retailer's cut

"Can you think of any experiments that you can run right now, before your product is ready, which would help you de-risk those assumptions?" asked Samantha.

"Well, for starters, we could approach merchandisers at a number of retailers to see if they would commit to carrying our ball once it was finished. That would inform us on #1 and #2. Frankly, it would also get us specifics on how much they control pricing and how big a cut they are going to want to take, which feeds into #6." said Simon.

"I think we could also test consumer demand and purchase conversion rates through a landing page or a crowdfunding campaign," said Das. "Those kinds of experiments could help us understand consumer price sensitivity, which also would help us understand our profit potential or risk."

"What if we looked for latent consumer demand by examining google search frequency?" said Simon. "And we could test for interest in this concept by running a wave of Google or Facebook ads and measuring click-through rates. Or we could even set up an online store, but mark the ball as sold out, and see if people will sign up for a waiting list."

"Good. I think you're starting to realize that there are a lot of quick ways to more concretely inform your business model," said Samantha. "You'll want to flesh out the priorities and specifics after our meeting, but notice that absolutely none of these experiments require you to have a finished product!"

She continued, "Since we're on a roll, let's brainstorm the other revenue model you found interesting. What if your real business was the software that came with the ball, and you charged for hosting the data or providing some sort of analytical and training tools? What risk assumptions do you see there?"

After a short exercise, they had a new list:

Hypothesis: we sell the ball cheaply (or free?) to college coaches, and they subscribe to an app that hosts the data and helps them analyze it
Risky assumptions:

1. College coaches will want to pay for our data and tools

2. Coaches have the budget, or budget flexibility, to pay for our data tools

3. We can make enough money from subscription fees to cover the cost of the business and the ball

4. Related to #3, coaches find the data useful enough that they continue subscribing for a long time

5. We can build a direct sales force that sells to coaches at a profit

"Now I'm going to ask you the same question as before," Samantha said. "How could you test these risky assumptions starting today?"

"We've been interviewing them about how they coach their players and their interest in this idea, but we haven't really talked about how much money they have to spend, how they decide what to spend it on, or if they have any current budget for training or data tools. That might expose challenges in selling them," said Simon.

"I agree," said Das, "But I also think that we could take it even further and try to sell them. We could have an experiment where we try to sell at least 50% of the coaches we pitch."

"But how do we sell something that isn't even finished?" said Simon.

"That's not as much of a blocker as you might think," said Samantha. "You could try to sell pre-orders. Or if that doesn't work, you can ask them to sign something non-binding that indicates their interest in making the purchase once the product is complete. What you want to do is get a purchase decision out of the realm of vague speculation and make it more concrete. You want them to really think about whether they could and would make this purchase. Keep in mind that a non-binding letter of intent is not the same thing as actual cash in your hand. I've seen entrepreneurs collect promises but struggle to convert those to orders. Still, if you think that's the right tactic, it's better than nothing."

"OK, so we need to figure out a method to pre-sell," said Simon. "I also suppose that we could test risks #1 and #2 with similar ideas to what we had for testing consumer demand. We could build a landing page, run ads, or run a crowdfunding campaign, but for this purpose customize the value props and targeting at coaches, not players."

"But how would we test risk #4?" he continued. "We can't know how long they will subscribe if we don't have the actual product in their hands over a period of months."

"True, you won't definitively know your churn rate until your product is in market," said Samantha, "But you definitely can get a solid look into whether you are on or off target. Remember the 'Wizard of Oz' experiment we discussed where you fake the ball and the data reports? Well, instead of measuring pre-orders from the players, you could instead run it aimed at the coaches. Give them the reports for a couple of weeks and then see if they agree to pay to continue the service, or get additional tools, at the end."

"If we run a test like that, we might also get a sense for how much we can charge and how hard the sales cycle might be," said Das. "That would inform our assumptions around how expensive a sales force we need, how long sales cycles might run, and how much revenue we could realistically expect in the early days. If we plug those into a simple financial model, that would help us build an initial answer to risk #5."

Samantha leaned back in her chair. "You've got a ton of homework, but that's the nature of startups," she said. "Let's meet again in three weeks. In the meantime, I highly recommend that you get out and talk to some industry experts, so that you understand your options and your market a little bit better. Don't try to run all your experiments at once. Prioritize one that you can get going immediately. Fill out your experiment template, get going, and then expand from there. When we next meet, I expect you to have a lot more concrete data from the market. I promise you, you'll be glad for it."

KEY TAKEAWAYS

Here are a few useful takeaways from this story:

1. Don't get so caught up in building and testing your product that you forget to pay attention to who your initial target customer should be, how you will acquire them, how you will make money, and what your sales and fulfillment costs will be.

2. If you have a preferred revenue model, have the team come together to expose and define your risky assumptions.

3. There are almost always creative ways to test those risky assumptions faster and sooner than most people think. When you ask yourself, "how can I learn about this starting today," you might be surprised at how creative you can get.

4. Don't try to test a menu of business model options. Both businesses and experiments need focus. As we discussed in the chapter "Starting with First Principles", first you should identify your current set of beliefs around your business model, then prioritize the risks, and then dive into experiment design and execution.

Experiment Archetypes

"Covert efforts can only reveal so much. At some point, ideas have to be tested in the wild."

JEFF GOTHELF & JOSH SEIDEN
Authors of *Sense and Respond* and *Lean UX*

For those new to experiments, it is useful to picture some of the many types and variations of experiments that you could run. While the list that follows is far from comprehensive, it should get you started. We've tried to cover some of the most common variations and included specific tips for each.

TESTING DEMAND

LANDING PAGE TESTS

A landing page test is where you create a simple web page (or website) that expresses your value proposition and gives the visitor the ability to express their interest with some sort of call to action. Your call to action might be submitting an email, filling out a form, or even entering a credit card number (as long as you do that securely). When Tuft and Needle, which makes and sells mattresses online, started out, the co-founders literally took a photograph of a mattress, created a landing page with their value proposition and a credit card form, and drove traffic to it to see if anyone would make a purchase. They intentionally broke the credit card integration so that money wouldn't process, while still allowing them to measure the activity. The results gave them the confidence to move forward. Tuft and Needle was acquired in 2018 after surpassing $250M in annual revenue.

One consideration is how soft to make your call to action. This will affect how you interpret your results. For example, it's easy for someone to give you their email address, but another thing altogether if someone thinks that they are spending money. Remember that this is a learning exercise, not a marketing exercise. You aren't necessarily trying to make it as easy as possible for visitors to convert, but rather trying to measure how much they want something. Sometimes having your landing page visitors jump through an extra hoop gives you a stronger signal.

Another important consideration is whether you make your landing page on-brand or whether you hide your brand. Established companies sometimes find it easier to test out new ideas off-brand in order to take more risk, duck bureaucratic hurdles, and also not confuse the market. You'll also want to think about how to handle the potential bait-and-switch problem of implying that a product is real and then having to tell people that it isn't. This is less of an issue for startups, but in the case of the *Cooking Light* example, that landing page was on-brand and we didn't want to sully that brand with a bait-and-switch. Our solution was to pretend that there was a paid trial, state that it was full, and then to ask people to sign up for the waiting list.

Landing pages present an interesting opportunity to test different price points or product bundles, but just be cautious not to present too many options to your visitor. As with all experiments,

Your Diet Could Look Like This

Lose Weight and Love Every Bite

The Editors of Cooking Light Magazine present a new program that makes healthy eating a delightful lifestyle, rather than a sacrifice.

You can customize delicious weekly meal plans for you and your family, knowing that you are in the care of our professional chefs and dietitians.

Imagine a diet that never gets boring. Now stop imagining, join our fast-growing community, and take a leap into a healthier, tastier life.

Sign up today →

Your Delicious Diet Plan

✓ Start losing fast
  Our two-week jumpstart plan will get you losing—and get you loving your plan!

✓ Weekly meal plans based on your weight-loss goal
  Breakfast, lunch, dinner, snacks—at home or out—we've got you covered.

Fried Egg BLT Sandwich (341 calories)

> CookingLight
>
> Cooking Light is America's #1 food magazine with 25+ years of expertise in making healthy recipes taste great. Our dietitians and chefs created this large collection of best kitchen-approved recipes in existence.

$18 ^{99}

6 month trial

Limited Trial Program (FULL)
Join the waiting list below

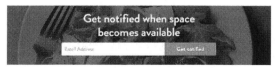

Get notified when space becomes available

Email Address   Get notified

Example: the initial landing page used in the Cooking Light Diet experiment (some content has been cropped)

if you have too many changing variables, it becomes very hard to interpret the results.

There are existing services that make it easy to create a landing page. Unbounce, Instapage and LeadPages are just a few of many options, but you can also use one of the many visual web-page builders out there (Tilda, Wix, SquareSpace, etc). However, if you're technically savvy and want full control over how your landing page looks, it's pretty easy to roll your own.

Tip: a warning: don't present a bunch of options at the same time to a visitor and ask them to pick their favorite. If you want to test different options, then it's better to A/B test these across different users rather than present them all at once.

ADVERTISING TESTS

Advertising tests are nothing more than boiling your value proposition down to something that can be presented to a targeted audience to see if they convert. Commonly used advertising platforms include Google AdWords, Facebook ads, and Craigslist. You will likely want to A/B test variations on your value proposition, as well as explore different channels. Ultimately you will have two conversion points to measure: the ad itself, and then wherever the ad takes the user, which is often a landing page or a survey.

Tip: start with a small amount of money and optimize your ad settings based on the initial results before expanding your spend. In particular, be cautious with the "match type" of your keywords. If you select "broad match", you might find yourself paying for a lot of irrelevant clicks.

PROMOTIONAL TESTS

A variation of an advertising test is to produce some sort of digital or physical promotional material to get feedback on your value proposition, or even more powerfully, to see if you can generate demand. Dropbox provides one of the most famous examples of a promotional test. Everyone told them the storage market was commoditized and impossible to enter. Before they started building their product, they created a short demo video that explained their proposed solution and asked people to sign up for a waiting list. The response was tremendous (their waiting list jumped from 5,000 to 75,000). It gave them the confidence to invest in the heavy engineering work required.

You need to match the production quality to your audience. Dropbox was aiming at a geeky audience and their low production quality was viewed as humorous and charming. In another segment, say the fashion industry, the Dropbox style would never have worked. You also need to really nail both the value proposition and the narrative.

Tip: promotional tests are definitely cheaper than building a product, but getting the story-telling and form factor right usually takes some testing unto itself.

PRE-SELLING (INCLUDING CROWD-FUNDING)

An idea probably as old as mankind, pre-selling is simply where you try to book orders before you actually have the product. For consumer products, you can do this manually one customer at a time, but a scalable alternative is to use crowdfunding platforms (for example Kickstarter or Indiegogo). However, keep in mind that using those platforms creates a strong obligation to deliver.

For enterprise products, pre-selling can be as simple as you getting out there and directly signing up early customers. There are a few different ways to handle this. In some cases, you literally can get people to pay you before the product is done. This not only gives you a strong signal for demand, but also is a marvelous way to fund a business. But in other situations you will be forced to get potential customers to sign up for a pilot program, or sign a non-binding "letter of intent" that expresses the willingness to pay once a product is ready. The more you are trying to test your pricing model and customer willingness to buy, the more you should steer towards pre-purchases and paid pilots.

A variation on pre-selling, for those expecting to be reliant on channel partners for customer acquisition, is to try to land early channel partnership commitments, as long as they are not so loose as to be meaningless.

Tip: if you are doing customer discovery at the same time as trying to pre-sell, then spend the first part of your meetings listening and learning, and save the sales pitch for the end.

TESTING PRODUCT/FEATURES

PAPER TESTING / PAPER MOCKUPS

Paper tests are where you mock up an example of an application user interface or report and put them in front of a potential customer. This applies primarily to software products, such as mobile and web applications, and information products such as data, analysis, and media. These tests don't literally need to be on paper, but can be images on an iPad or an email. This was a component in Das and Simon's larger experiment in the initial story. They were able to get better feedback by putting something specific in the hands of potential customers. Because paper mockups are not experiential, you have to take results with a grain of salt, but you can still learn interesting things.

When creating a paper mockup that works across a user journey, with multiple steps or screens, make sure you story-board out your narrative and flow first so the whole thing holds together.

Tip: paper testing tends not to work well for things that are highly dynamic, such as whether a search engine is returning the right results. A paper test can tell you whether a user understands the way you have laid information out on the screen, but not whether the dynamic results of a search query are good or bad. For that, you would need a prototype or wizard-of-oz test.

BUTTON / DOOR TO NOWHERE

A "button to nowhere" is also particularly applicable to websites and software products. It is where you dangle a feature in front of users before you have actually built it. For example, if you want to know if users care about personalizing their experience, you could put a button that says "Personalize" in a relevant part of your application, and measure how many people click it. Once clicked, usually the user then sees a pop-up window that explains that the feature is not yet ready (or even better, asks them if they would be willing to be interviewed about their interest in the feature). Note that this approach doesn't literally have to use a button. Choose the right UX design for your needs.

Tip: be careful that you don't irritate users with too many "bait and switch" situations. Write respectful copy and don't over-use this experiment type.

TASK COMPLETION

Sometimes an experiment is as simple as seeing if someone completes a task. In one experiment, we left cards on chairs at a conference to see if people would fill them out and return them. In another, we ambushed doctors in the hallway to see if they could readily complete a task on their mobile phones.

Here is a more complex example of a "task completion" experiment: a product team for a successful B2B marketplace wanted to add user-level profiles to their application, similar to what you see on LinkedIn or Facebook. They believed that this new feature, if broadly adopted, would lift both user engagement and revenue. To test for interest, they chose 30 users and emailed them each a partially completed user profile template (an Excel file). In the email, they explained that user-level profiles were coming to the site, and asked each recipient to review the attachment, fill in the blank information, correct erroneous information, and send it back. They set their success target at 20 completed responses and received back 25. This gave them the confidence to invest the engineering effort.

Tip: to run a sharp, tactical task completion experiment, make sure you are working off of a good hypothesis statement. Keep a critical eye during the experiment design process to make the believability and thus usefulness of the data as strong as possible.

PRODUCT PROTOTYPES

A prototype is a working version of your product that is built for learning and fast iteration, rather than for robustness or scale. With a physical product, it might be a hand-made or 3D-printed version of something (or part of something) that you eventually want to manufacture at scale. In software, this might be a working, even partial, version of a feature hacked together with code, a prototyping tool, a form builder, etc.

Prototypes can be big or little. Before Apple jumped into retail, the company created a full-scale prototype of an Apple store. This allowed them to test and evolve their ideas around layout, product display, and visitor movement — all before building the first store for real. Similarly, Starwood Hotels built out prototypes of their Aloft hotel lobbies before starting construction for real.

Game designers have long created simple prototypes to test out game rules and play dynamics before investing in high fidelity digital or physical product creation. We worked with one team that tested out their digital game concept with index cards and printouts. They used their crude prototype to test whether their game was fun when played more than once. They also wanted to test and iterate the game design before investing in software code, which is malleable but significantly more expensive to change.

Prototypes aren't always necessary. In the case of Das and Simon, they skipped building a prototype and instead faked their soccer ball.

Tip: don't confuse building your prototype with building your real product. Take on a hacker's mindset, and don't worry about the re- usability of software code or materials. Instead, focus on the speed and quality of what you can learn.

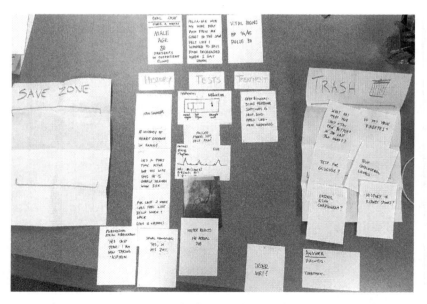

Example: a paper prototype of a learning game for doctors, created to test a concept prior to building a digital version.

WIZARD OF OZ TESTS

A Wizard of Oz test is where the customer thinks they are interfacing with a real product, but where your team provides the service in a manual way, hidden behind the scenes (hence the name). This allows you to put a fake version of the product into the hands of a customer very quickly and adjust the service offering with flexibility. The opening story with Das and Simon was a Wizard of Oz test. So was the two-week meal plan experiment in the *Cooking Light* example.

Wizard of Oz tests have to be both planned and run with careful attention to details in order for the manual work to stay hidden behind the curtain. You'll likely want to use a tool to keep the team and activities organized and tracked (examples of useful organizing tools include Trello and Asana).

In addition, we've often found it useful to automate some of the manual tasks. Sometimes this can be done by cobbling together online or open source tools. In the *Cooking Light* example, we invested a day coding a simple tool to automate the process of getting our recipes into an attractively formatted email. This saved us countless hours of unnecessary grunt work.

Tip: always do an abbreviated trial run before starting a Wizard of Oz test. It will help you understand how many participants you can handle, and inevitably expose ways you can improve the experiment.

CONCIERGE TESTS

A concierge test is where you manually, and overtly, act as the product you eventually want to build (unlike a Wizard of Oz where people are behind the scenes). For example, if you wanted to build a product that was an automated personal shopper, you would hire yourself out as a personal shopper and while delivering your consulting service, you could test your ideas for a superior customer experience.

Rent the Runway, a New York-based startup, used a concierge experiment to successfully test whether women would actually rent dresses. They provided an in-person service to female college students where the students could try on a dress before renting it. The startup My Wellbeing wanted to test their idea for matching patients with therapists. Instead of rushing to build product, they first played match-maker by giving both sides a form to fill out and then manually connecting the two sides. In doing so, they not only were able to test out the value of their service, they learned how to make better matches. Non-profit Taproot Foundation did exactly the same thing to test a digital marketplace that matched non-profits with volunteer experts and service providers.

Tip: One advantage of concierge tests, since you're acting in a consultative capacity, is that you get to talk directly with your customers. This can really maximize your qualitative learning. Furthermore, it is often easier to charge money for the work.

PILOTS

When you run a pilot, you put an early version of your product in the hands of your customers, but you scale down the size of the implementation and put a finite time period on the project. The term "pilot" is more commonly used in the enterprise (B2B) space where testing a product takes more effort and requires the involvement of more people. It takes a lot more effort and investment on your side to run a pilot compared to a Wizard of Oz or Concierge test, simply because you need more of your product built. However, the lines get blurry — to run an early pilot, you might still be manually compensating for some unfinished parts of your product.

There are three reasons to do pilots. The first is tied to the pre-selling archetype listed above. In this case, your goal is to see whether customers care enough about your problem and solution to give you both time and money. Some teams are able to charge their full intended price for a pilot, but most end up giving pilot customers a discount. We believe in the benefits of paid, rather than free, pilots. Even getting a small amount of money is a strong, positive signal, and not merely because of the money. It's also because corporate buyers usually have to go through procurement approval processes. You might be thinking, "but won't that make it harder to get pilots?" The answer is yes, but remember that sometimes intentional friction is beneficial if your real goal is testing is the intensity of customer demand.

The other two reasons to run a pilot are less about experiments, but still powerful to your business and worth mentioning. Pilots are a great way to build early customer references, which will make future sales much easier. Lastly, they provide invaluable early feedback for your product design, without waiting for everything about your business to be fully baked. While in this book we constantly stress how much you need to think about your business, not just your product, the fact is that both need to work for you to succeed.

Tip: do your best to charge money for your pilot, and run your pilots in a way that you can learn as much as possible on as many dimensions as possible.

USABILITY TESTING

Many of the experiments in this book are about testing for value, desirability and marketability, but it is also important to test for usability and viability. A usability test checks whether someone can someone effectively use a product without getting stuck or blocked. Usability failures can be design flaws (example: "I can't find the button!") or more systemic challenges (example: "doctors in remote parts of Africa can't access our app because mobile Internet is too slow and unstable")

Usability tests are actually a bit easier to run, because you don't need as large a sample set. As a matter of fact, usability expert Jakob Nielsen, of the Nielsen Norman Group, calculated that five people is the optimal number to test.

Tip: If you're working on a software application, I highly recommend Stephen Krug's book Rocket Surgery Made Easy to learn how to approach practical usability tests.

THE POSSIBILITIES ARE ENDLESS

Not every experiment fits neatly into the above archetypes. It's more important to be practical than to try to neatly fit into a single experiment archetype. Coming up with sharp experiments just takes creativity and a nose for what will give you believable information.

Avoiding Blockers and Building a Culture of Experimentation

"If we can get processes decentralized so that we can do a lot of experiments without it being very costly, we'll get a lot more innovation."

JEFF BEZOS

In our experience, once startups and execution teams get a taste for experiments, they want to do more. If you're going to spend months or years of your life on something new, which comes with risk, then you usually want to increase the odds that it matters.

In our experience, resistance to experiments tends to come from the top: the startup CEO who is lost in their own reality distortion field, or the large company executive, used to command-and-control, passing down detailed directions rather than setting goals and getting out of the way. To an executive who is used to saying, "go build this," an experiment feels like a distraction. By the time everyone realizes that the original idea isn't going to work, the command-and-control executive has swept it under the rug and is on to the next thing.

If your organization has resistance to experiments, we've seen two ways for this to change.

The first is a change of heart at the very top. The CEO (or senior executive) realizes that the success rate for new initiatives is way too low. They then try to force a culture of experimentation onto the organization. This is usually well received by the execution teams. However, middle management often resists because it pushes decision-making power lower in the organization. With training, patience, building from small wins to big ones, and consistent pressure from the CEO, you can break through corporate resistance to change.

The second is a humble grass-roots movement, where execution teams sneak experiments in where they can, and gradually start to co-opt management. As you chalk up little wins that lead to bigger wins, and as you story-tell your process, other teams will want to emulate you. The culture of experimentation will start to spread.

In some companies, you can find yourself blocked by either sales or legal/compliance. In the case of sales, the source of the problem is usually a desire for control over customer relationships. In most cases this can be resolved by creating ground rules over which customers/prospects you can reach directly versus needing to get advance permission. It always helps to connect your desire to run experiments with how it will directly benefit sales. If you are truly at loggerheads with a sales leader, you might need to appeal further up the hierarchy.

Opposition from compliance and legal departments can be trickier. Sometimes their concerns are real, grounded in true regulatory constraints and risk. However, those groups can take their desire to protect the business so far that they hamstring a company's ability to innovate. You have three options: go through, go around, or go outside. To go through the group, you need to first deeply understand the compliance concerns and risks, and then find a business-friendly leader within the blocking group. Then you can strike a compromise and document experiment-friendly ground rules. In most cases, the higher up you go, the more business-friendly you will find people, simply because senior executives are thinking more about the bigger picture. If that is impossible, you need to find and win over a business leader who has the power to overrule compliance or force a compromise. Lastly, you can try to start running experiments in more of an arms-length way, using external resources or even incorporating an external entity, but again you'll need a friend on your company's legal team to navigate these waters.

HELPING YOUR CASE

If you're a team that doesn't want to wait for a mindset shift at the top to run experiments, there are a few things to keep in mind that will increase your odds of success.

- Be very practical: Not everything needs an experiment. Focus on the big risks and your true end goals. Focus on keeping experiments as small and tight as possible.
- Be respectful: Look ahead to where you might run afoul of other groups (especially sales, account management, or customer success), and then be smart with your communications with those groups. You don't necessarily need to allow those groups to be bottlenecks. You can avoid headaches by getting them on board early, or at minimum, making sure that you're not messing up someone else's plans.
- Start with small wins: Begin building corporate appreciation for experiments in smaller, more tactical projects, and aggregate the successes into a larger narrative. Don't run big, expensive experiments that risk a splashy failure.
- Co-opt management: As we discussed in the chapter on Learning & Decisions, pull key management "stakeholders" into your regular decision meetings, and don't be afraid to empower

them to make decisions. That way, your process and your learning becomes their process and their learning.

- Externalize your work: It's important to control your own narrative, otherwise people will come up with their own. Share what you've learned, how you have learned it, and why you learned it. Always draw a connection back to the big goals. To do this, you could spin up an internal blog, do a "roadshow" to other teams, or run what we call a science fair.

RUNNING A SCIENCE FAIR

A science fair, at least in the context of this book, is an event where you share the essence of all your experimental work with your colleagues, not just showing them what you learned but also teaching them the methods for how you learned. The idea originally came from Jeff Patton, and was further developed by Jeff Gothelf and Josh Seiden, all brilliant thinkers on the processes behind great products.

At the Mayo Clinic, after 7 weeks of testing new ideas for continuing education for doctors, we ran a science fair in Rochester, MN, and invited many others in the organization to attend. We took over a room and coated the walls with paper, like a giant kindergarten craft project. We created a journey around the room that started with the project's goals and the team's operating structure and principles. The narrative then explained how we came up with product ideas, how we tested the potential of those ideas, and what the results were. We showed off artifacts from real experiments, including live prototypes. We fearlessly talked about ideas that were killed, and why they were killed. We talked about the pressures and pros and cons of moving so fast. The science fair was a huge success, not just in helping people understand what we had done, but also inspiring them in a new way of working.

At Auto Trader UK, we ran 11 cross-functional product teams

(engineers, designers, product managers, marketers) through a week-long bootcamp where they were all kicked out of the building to do research and run experiments against their current work initiatives. Some ideas got killed, some got reinforced, some big new opportunities were discovered, and everyone got to know the customer a whole lot better. At the end of the week, we had each team create a science fair display showing off their goals, their experiments, what they learned and any decisions that followed. We then invited the rest of the company in for a "happy hour" (indeed, beers were served). We even ran a competition where the company got to vote for the "best team" across several different categories. Like with The Mayo Clinic, it was a huge success, full of energy and enthusiasm. Preparing for the science fair forced the teams to really reflect on what they had done and learned. Delivering the science fair gave them an opportunity to feel tremendous pride in their hard work, and allowed the rest of the company to be inspired by it.

Done right, science fairs can spread infectious energy for running experiments. They are a tool not just to help you create a narrative around your activities, but also to take the concepts of customer discovery and experiments out of the realm of theory. Through examples, the principles become real, in full living color.

10 TIPS FOR RUNNING A SUCCESSFUL SCIENCE FAIR

1. Give attendees a taste of your journey, not just your results. Share what you learned along the way, as well as the decisions you made.
2. Be transparent about the good and bad. Don't sweep the (inevitable) mistakes under the rug because it's all part of the learning process.
3. Keep your presentation materials informal, rather than glossy and polished. This will anchor attendees in the speed, creativity and scrappiness of the process.

4. Create "immersion" moments for your attendees by letting them play with a prototype, or letting them experience being interviewed.

5. Spread out your team to act as guides and hosts.

6. Bring in snacks and add a touch of fun.

7. Choose your time of day wisely to maximize attendance. Don't create too wide a time window to attend, but instead try to concentrate attendance and energy. If it helps with attendance, you can even repeat your science fair at a second time.

8. Advertise the event and directly recruit people to attend. At Mayo, the team printed flyers and visited groups in person to encourage them to attend.

9. If you are part of a "heads-down" culture, recruit the CEO or a senior executive to email about the event, thus tacitly giving both permission and approval for people to take a few minutes away from work to attend.

10. As a follow-on, do site-visits to mentor other teams that express interest in working this way.

In Conclusion

*"I believe the best managers acknowledge and make room for what they
do not know - not just because humility is a virtue but because until
one adopts that mindset, the most striking breakthroughs cannot occur."*
ED CATMULL
CEO of Pixar

Breaking new ground always comes with risk. It doesn't really
matter whether you are trying to create a new company, lead a major
initiative, or release an important new product feature. Innovation
of any kind comes with uncertainty. We believe in leaning into that
uncertainty.

If you are like most, you are doing three things at once. You
are trying to (1) figure out how move as fast as possible, while (2)
making the most with limited resources, while also (3) trying to
increase your odds for success. We hope this book helps you in a
meaningful way across all three, but particularly the last.

To wrap things up, we want to leave you with a few final pieces
of advice. The first is to encourage you to stay practical at all times.
People tend to go awry with startup advice, whether "lean startup"
or other approaches, when they either get too dogmatic and try
to copy a playbook too literally, or when they just "try a bunch of

stuff" in a chaotic fashion. Neither extreme is wise. When it comes to experiments, you need to always use your judgment as to when to run one, how to run one, and when and how to make decisions from one.

Don't forget that as your business grows and changes, so too will your customer base. Keep on reality-checking your hypotheses. Keep on talking to and testing with humans. Whatever you are working on, Frank and I wish you the very best success.

Here is a final summary of key points from the book to help you conquer experimentation:

12 TIPS FOR RUNNING EFFECTIVE EXPERIMENTS

1. Save your experiment effort for risks that will truly impact the success or failure of your project or business.

2. Don't just think about experiments for your product. Remember to examine your customer segments, value propositions, customer acquisition methods, pricing plans and revenue models, unit economics, etc.

3. Stretch your thinking at the start because there are always more ways to test something than you think.

4. Be disciplined about the details because sloppy experiments lead to sloppy results.

5. Set target pass/fail goals ahead of time or you'll be tempted to rationalize what happened after the fact.

6. Ask how you can just learn just as much, if not more, with half the time and effort.

7. Optimize for learning, not for building product, or you'll move too slowly.

8. For big experiments, do a trial run first because you'll often discover things to improve.

9. Run your experiments with intensity and speed, because time will disappear faster than you think.

10. Include opportunities for qualitative research (talking to humans!) as you go.

11. Fight your own confirmation biases. In other words, don't twist results to hear what you want to hear, or dismiss undesirable results too quickly.

12. Combine evidence and judgment to make smart decisions (consider running weekly decision meetings) and execute!

PART FOUR

Appendix

"Waiting for perfect is never as smart as making progress."

SETH GODIN

Business Assumptions Exercise

If you are finding yourself getting stuck with the different business model canvases, you can use this series of questions to break out your key assumptions. Try to make your answers as concise and specific as possible.:

My target customer will be?
(Tip: how would you describe your primary target customer)

The problem my customer wants to solve is?
(Tip: what does your customer struggle with or what need do they want to fulfill)

My customer's need can be solved with?
(Tip: give a very concise description / elevator pitch of your product and how it addresses your target customer's problem)

Why can't my customer solve this today?
(Tip: what are the obstacles that have prevented my customer from solving this already)

The measurable outcome my customer wants to achieve is?
(Tip: what quantifiable change in your your customer's life makes them love your product)

My primary customer acquisition tactic will be?
(Tip: you will likely have multiple marketing channels, but there is often one method, at most two, that dominates your customer acquisition – what is your current guess)

My earliest adopter will be?
(Tip: remember that you can't get to the mainstream customer without getting early adopters first)

I will make money (revenue) by?
(Tip: don't list all the ideas for making money, but pick your primary one)

My primary competition will be?
(Tip: think about both direct and indirect competition, including substitutes your customer can use to address their problem)

I will beat my competitors primarily because of?
(Tip: what truly differentiates you from the competition?)

My biggest risk to financial viability is?
(Tip: what could prevent you from getting to breakeven? is there something baked into your revenue or cost model that you can de-risk?)

My biggest technical or engineering risk is?
(Tip: is there a major technical challenge that might hinder building your product?)

Finally, answer the following open-ended question. Be creative and really examine your points of failure.

What assumptions do we have that, if proven wrong, would cause this business to fail?

1.

2.

3.

4.

5.

6.

7.

8.

9.

10.

11.

12.

After you have looked at your business holistically and also answered the broad final question, mark the assumptions that would have a large impact on your business **and** feel highly uncertain. Now you know your priorities for customer discovery and the experiments you need to run!

Note: you can find a pdf of this exercise on talkingtohumans.com.

Working with a Mentor

One of the more interesting questions that came back from the early feedback on this book was, "How do I find a Samantha of my own?" The answer is simple: mentors are out there, all you have to do is ask. It is astounding how rarely people actually ask. The startup community is incredibly generous by nature. You're missing out if you get so caught up in your own struggle that you don't look for a bit of experienced, external advice.

TIPS ON CHOOSING A MENTOR

- Look for someone with real and relevant experience, who has truly been through the fire.

- Describe the kind of person and experience you are looking for to your peers, and see who they recommend.

- Look at who is speaking at relevant meetups in your area, or who is sharing relevant advice online.

TIPS ON APPROACHING A MENTOR

- Research them first.

- If you can network your way to a warm intro, that is always the best approach. LinkedIn can be useful here. Second best: figure out a way to meet them in-person at an event, when you can ask for a follow-up conversation (tip: don't hog their time at the event). Lastly, go direct if you absolutely have to.

- Carefully write a thoughtful, personalized, but still concise note as to who you are, where you want advice, and why them.

- Don't ask up-front for a recurring mentorship relationship. Just ask for an initial 30-minute meeting or call. Explain the kind of advice you are seeking, or even better, ask them a specific question about something you are struggling with.

- In getting that first meeting, don't be afraid to follow up and be a little persistent. People are busy and you won't be a priority (at first). That said, most people are thankful for polite follow-up as long as you space it out (i.e. not three days in a row), and make it easy for them to gracefully say no.

- If they do say no, don't give up, but keep on looking.

- Go into your initial meeting with a specific problem or challenge where you want their input. Don't wing it.

- Kick off your initial meeting with a thank you for the time and a very concise intro explaining your context. Then ask them a question to give them a chance to speak. Hopefully the meeting quickly turns into a healthy, organic back-and-forth.

- If each mentoring session goes well, ask to meet again. If the connection becomes strong enough in this meeting or the next, ask if they would be open to making your advice sessions a regular thing.

TIPS FOR WORKING WITH A MENTOR

- Work to their schedule and make it easy to schedule time. You might even try putting a recurring event on your mutual calendars to minimize the back-and-forth each time, however don't be surprised if you're constantly rescheduling. That's just life.

- Go into your mentoring sessions with a plan about the

things you want to share and discuss. Even better, share that list with your mentor ahead of the meeting.

- Be honest and open with what and how you share. If you don't get real about the hard stuff, they won't be able to help.

- Don't get defensive. Be open to being challenged.

- Don't just follow the advice of your mentor blindly. They aren't your boss. They aren't in your shoes. They might be an exceptional business person, but they won't know all of your context. Listen to what they say, poke at it afterwards and examine it from multiple sides, but remember that the responsibility for good decisions is ultimately yours.

- If it's not working for either side, don't force it.

THE MAKE UP OF A GOOD MENTOR

- They are empathetic, not judgmental.

- They are focused on you when you meet.

- They ask good questions and create options for you to think about, rather than giving you a single prescriptive path to follow.

- They make (enough) time for you and are not impossible to schedule.

References in the Book

QUOTE HEADERS

Introductory quote by Richard Feynman: Cornell Lecture, 1964

Story: Steve Blank, *Ardent 2: Get Out of My Building*, October 8, 2009, https://steveblank.com/2009/10/08/get-out-of-my-building/

The Why and the How: quote attributed to Thomas Edison

Why We Run (and Don't Run) Experiments: Eric Ries, *The Lean Startup*, Crown Business, 2011 (Lean Startup is trademarked by Eric Ries)

Starting with Principles: Richard Feynman, *Cargo Cult Science*, Caltech's 1974 commencement address

What Makes a Good Experiment: David Bland, excerpted from https://twitter.com/davidjbland/status/302138756813684736

The Anatomy of an Experiment: quote attributed to Eisenhower by Richard Nixon in *Six Crises*, Doubleday, 1962

The Template in Practice: Steve Blank, *Faith-Based versus Fact-Based Decision Making*, June 5, 2009, https://steveblank.com/2009/06/05/faith-based-versus-fact-based-decision-making/

Generating and Refining Experiments: excerpt from Melissa Perri, *Finding the Truth Behind MVPs*, May 5, 2016, https://melissaperri.com/blog/2016/05/05/finding-the-truth-behind-mvps

Learning and Decisions: quote attributed to Jim Barksdale

Important Considerations: quote attributed to Steve Jobs

Testing the Business vs Testing the Product: Ash Maurya, *Love the Problem, Not Your Solution*, August 11, 2016, https://blog.leanstack.com/love-the-problem-not-your-solution-65cfbfb1916b

Experiment Archetypes: Jeff Gothelf and Josh Seiden, *Sense and Respond*, Harvard Business Review Press, Febuary 2017

Avoiding Blockers and Building a Culture of Experimentation: Jeff Bezos, quoted in The Innovator's DNA, Harvard Business Review, December 2009, https://hbr.org/2009/12/the-innovators-dna

Conclusion: Ed Catmull, *Creativity, Inc.*, Random House, April 2014.

Appendix: Seth Godin, Take what you can get (?), November 7, 2009. https://seths.blog/2009/11/take-what-you-can-get

ADDITIONAL QUOTES / REFERENCES

Starting with First Principles

Mark Suster, Are Business Plans Still Necessary?, Nov 3, 2009, https://bothsidesofthetable.com/are-business-plans-still-necessary-ef8fffd5dbff

The Anatomy of an Experiment and Experiment Archetypes

Jakob Nielsen, Why You Only Need to Test with 5 Users, March 19, 2000, https://www.nngroup.com/articles/why-you-only-need-to-test-with-5-users/

Learning and Decisions

Bill Aulet, *Disciplined Entrepreneurship*, Wiley, July 2013.

Other Learning Resources

AUTHORS

The seminal books on the topics of lean innovation and customer development are Steve Blank and Bob Dorf's *The Startup Owner's Manual* and Eric Ries' *The Lean Startup* and its sequel *The Startup Way*. If you are interested in lean, we also recommend Ash Maurya's two books *Running Lean* and *Scaling Lean*, and *The Lean Entrepreneur*, by Brant Cooper and Patrick Vlaskovits.

If you are interested in changing culture at a larger organization, we recommend *Sense and Respond*, by Jeff Gothelf and Josh Seiden. If you are working on a product team, we also recommend their book *Lean UX*, Melissa Perri's book *The Build Trap*, and Jeff Patton's *User Story Mapping*.

There are a ton of other resources out there, from books to videos and blog posts. Rather than link to particular items and thus miss out on newer developments, here are a few names that we recommend you pay attention to in addition to the above: Alex Osterwalder, Alistair Croll, Barry O'Reilly, Ben Yoskowitz, Cindy Alvarez, David Bland, Laura Klein, and Tristan Kromer.

OUR WEBSITE

On our website testingwithhumans.com, you can get worksheet pdfs and sign up for our email list. If you are interested in learning more about customer discovery, you can get the book *Talking to Humans*, as well as accompanying worksheet pdfs, on our website talkingtohumans.com.

Behind the Book

Testing with Humans was written by Giff Constable, with the collaboration of Frank Rimalovski.

Giff Constable

Giff Constable (giffconstable.com) is a repeat entrepreneur who has sold three companies and helped build many others. In 2014, he wrote the award-winning book *Talking to Humans*, in partnership with Frank Rimalovski, which is now standard reading in university and accelerator programs around the world. He led the globally recognized innovation consulting firm Neo as CEO until its acquisition by Pivotal, and personally led major projects at the Mayo Clinic and Time Inc., among others. He has held product and business roles across multiple startups, and provided M&A and IPO services to technology firms while at Broadview/Jefferies. He tries to give back to the entrepreneurial community whenever possible. He lives outside of New York City with his wife and two children.

Frank Rimalovski

Frank Rimalovski is an early-stage investor and entrepreneurship educator with over 25 years of experience in technology commercialization, startups and venture capital investing. He is the founding executive director of New York University's Entrepreneurial Institute, and managing director of their Innovation Venture Fund. In 2014, he collaborated with Giff Constable to produce the award-winning book Talking to Humans. Frank currently serves as a mentor at TechStars, and teaches entrepreneurship at NYU's Courant Institute. He has previously taught at the Tandon School of Engineering, and as an Instructor in the NSF's I-Corps program, and has trained and mentored hundreds of entrepreneurs in customer development and lean startup methodologies. Previously, he was a founding partner of New Venture Partners, director/entrepreneur-in-residence at Lucent's New Ventures Group, and has held various positions in product management, marketing and business development at Sun Microsystems, Apple and NeXT. He lives outside of New York City with his wife and his increasingly mellow mutt.

page intentionally blank